END PAPERS: *Afternoon thunderstorm over Yosemite.*

A Contribution to the Heritage of Every American

A CONTRIBUTION TO
THE HERITAGE
OF EVERY AMERICAN

THE CONSERVATION ACTIVITIES
OF JOHN D. ROCKEFELLER, JR.

TEXT BY NANCY NEWHALL

PROLOGUE BY FAIRFIELD OSBORN

EPILOGUE BY HORACE MARDEN ALBRIGHT

 ALFRED A. KNOPF

NEW YORK

1957

Snake River and the Grand Tetons.

" . . . to encourage human conduct to sustain and enrich life on earth."

FROM "THE STATEMENT OF PURPOSES," THE CONSERVATION FOUNDATION

[FIRST EDITION]

COPYRIGHT 1957 BY THE CONSERVATION FOUNDATION
MANUFACTURED IN THE UNITED STATES OF AMERICA

CONTENTS

Prologue — by Fairfield Osborn   ix

PART ONE: PLACES NEAR HOME

Forest Hill Park   3

The Palisades   15

The Hudson Valley   29

PART TWO: NATIONAL PARKS

Acadia   47

Shenandoah   61

Great Smoky Mountains   71

Museums: Mesa Verde, Grand Canyon, Yellowstone   83

The Grand Tetons   101

Yosemite   115

Virgin Islands   127

PART THREE: TRIUMPHS OF NATURE AND OF MAN

The Redwoods   143

Colonial Williamsburg   155

Epilogue — by Horace Marden Albright   175

JOHN D. ROCKEFELLER, JR.

PROLOGUE

THIS is a story of a land and its people — and of a man who cherished both. It is a story without parallel in any other country on the face of the earth or in any other time in the history of man. It reveals events that, in magnitude and in kind, have not occurred before nor is there likelihood that they ever will again. Any such milestone in human affairs is the consequence of a combination of unusual circumstances. This story was written over a period of more than half a century as a result of a unique interplay of time, place and the vision of an individual.

The remarkable characteristics of the land itself contributed immeasurably to the unfolding of the story. It is true that Americans who visit other lands will discover mountains far higher, rivers mightier and longer, forests vaster, deserts more forbidding and extensive, historical relics of man's arts and labors more numerous and more ancient. However, the people of no other nation possess so varied and inclusive a combination of these natural and historical heritages. This fact the man perceived when he was still very young, and through this realization his vision was first born.

Time brought to him and his family the great wealth needed to convert the early vision into reality. He rejected the delusion that wealth was personal and turned his thoughts and energies toward discovering ways through which the fruits of wealth could be enjoyed by the greatest number of people. It is a wonderful and heartening fact that this attitude toward the responsibilities of private fortune has, to a large degree, become so prevalent and may indeed be said to have become characteristic of "the American way."

How can one measure any man's impulses and motivations? In one instance a contribution was given to insure the establishment of a National Park in the Great Smoky Mountains. "This gift," he once said, "was made as a memorial to the beautiful spirit of my mother." In another instance the

Teton Mountains in Wyoming stirred him deeply. He described them as "quite the grandest and most spectacular mountains I have ever seen . . . a picture of ever-changing beauty which is to me beyond compare." As a result of this profound personal experience, he at once set about purchasing land so that this incomparable region could be held in perpetual trust by the Federal Government for the benefit and enjoyment of all his fellow countrymen. Such depth of feeling and awe for the wonders of nature provided the vital urge for the preservation of regions of outstanding beauty which he realized, if once marred or destroyed, could never be replaced. Concurrently, the preservation of historical monuments became part of the whole broad plan culminating in what is perhaps the most notable task of restoration ever undertaken — that of Colonial Williamsburg.

These things were not easily done. Vision alone was not enough. Wealth alone was insufficient. Concept of the plan as a whole, arduous attention to detail and even passion for perfection, feeling for color and beauty, respect for working associates, talent for administration, patience and, lastly, tolerance of criticism and even of misunderstanding of purpose — all these qualities were brought into play, for all were essential to the fulfillment of the early vision.

How can these contributions to the life of the people of the United States be measured? It is not enough to say that at this very time over fifty million visits are made each year by Americans as well as people from far countries, gaining recreation, knowledge and inspiration in these places that are the result of his dedication. The years will roll on. Ever greater numbers of people will find benefit to body and spirit in these shrines of nature and history. Yet the vision remains, for it is beyond the mind of man to measure the essences that are the heritage of every American.

FAIRFIELD OSBORN

PART ONE: PLACES NEAR HOME

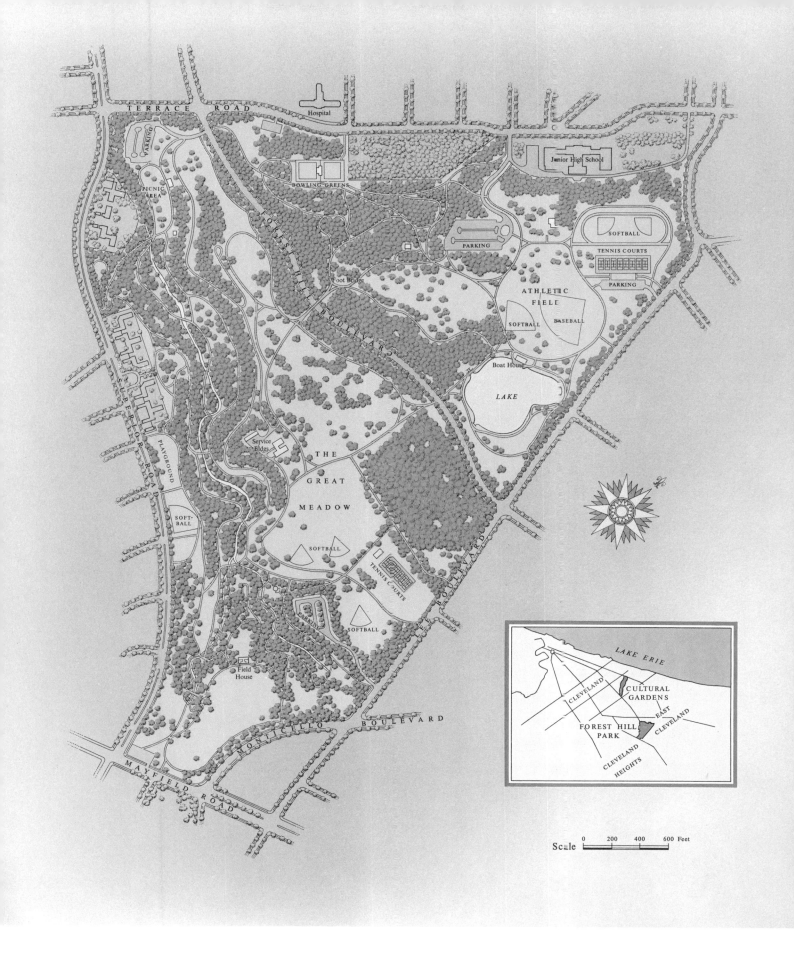

FOREST HILL PARK

FOREST HILL PARK today, like a green island in an urban sea, rises between the cities of East Cleveland and Cleveland Heights In 1873, when John D. Rockefeller, Sr., first climbed it and looked toward Lake Erie, he bought the wooded hilltop streaked by ravines as "a good investment." Seven years later the Forest Hill estate became the Rockefeller summer home. The young family christened it "The Homestead."

Here John D. Rockefeller, Jr., under his father's tutelage, first developed his lifelong interest in landscapes and road building. Under the old oaks his father planted a great lawn, and dammed a brook to make a lake, where his four children could learn to swim and handle a boat. He laid out a half-mile riding course. Through the ridges and down the ravines, he built more than six miles of drives and paths. When John, Jr., was sixteen, he assumed some of the responsibility for the supervision of Forest Hill. He cleared the underbrush, resurfaced the roads and planted scores of new trees among the old — doing much of the work himself. The practical knowledge acquired in those early years was to characterize all his subsequent activities in conservation projects. Until the house burned in 1917, the family considered Forest Hill their home. By then, the cities were closing in around it. On its eastern side the son later built a residential area; he gave other land for a school, a hospital, boulevards. Carrying out a hope of his father, in 1938 he gave its two hundred and sixty-six remaining acres to the cities, and ten thousand dollars to design it as a park.

Today the cities act jointly to adapt the Park to changing public needs. The drives are now broad walks. There are tennis courts, playgrounds, picnic groves, even bowling greens. Children and adults ramble through the wooded uplands and play on the Great Meadow. "I am delighted beyond expression," wrote John D. Rockefeller, Jr., "as I know my father would be . . . that the people of your community and the surrounding country will be able to enjoy for all time, as I did during the happy days of my childhood and youth, the beautiful area comprised within the Park."

Forest Hill roadway.

A park for recreation, Forest Hill lets everybody walk on the grass. Around Rockefeller Lake small boys sail model yachts and cast for minnows from the dock.

From the roof and porches of the long-vanished Homestead, Lake Erie could be seen in the distance. Inside, no curtain shut away the view.

AT THE HOMESTEAD, the Rockefellers lived simply. The children were brought up as their father had been — "to work, to save, and to give." They pulled weeds at ten for a penny, chopped wood and broke stone at fifteen cents an hour; and from such earnings each gave weekly to church and charity. Morning began with family prayers at 7:30; family attendance at church, Sunday school and prayer meeting was faithful. Music and the outdoors were the family's pleasures Picking wild strawberries in spring, chestnutting in fall, playing follow-the-leader on bicycles by moonlight, John, Jr., developed what he calls his "passionate awareness of the outdoor world." At sixteen he could build and plant so well that he was qualified beyond his years to assume some responsibility for the grounds at Forest Hill. Here he trained his eye to see how a place could be improved by better roadways and how a project might be completed in the future — an ability reflected years later in his conservation and restoration projects. In addition to developing this exceptional power of visualizing, he began to see also the value of conserving the beauties of the natural world and making them more accessible to more people. Of Forest Hill, the elder Rockefeller said, in 1920, he hoped "to perpetuate the character of Forest Hill as a park where people may go for rest and recreation and quiet walks through its ravines and along its winding roads and paths . . ."

Down the ravines grow the beeches, sugar maples, dogwood and shadblow, native to Ohio.

A colonnade of maples, which John D. Rockefeller, Jr., as a boy, planted to shade horses and drivers from the summer sun, now arches over this broad walk.

OF HIS BOYHOOD at Forest Hill, John D. Rockefeller, Jr., wrote, "I think perhaps I have always had an eye for nature. I remember as a boy loving sunsets . . . I remember the fairy forms of the trees when they shed their leaves. I remember what the sycamore trees looked like, and the maple trees. Every time I ride through the woods today, the smell of the trees — particularly when a branch has just been cut and the sap is running — takes me back to my early impressions in the woods."

To keep such impressions fresh and vivid for others down the generations, the native woodlands, brooks and meadows of Forest Hill have been preserved — as far as city conditions allow.

The Great Meadow, once the golf course, now serves as a playground for children.

Elm, oak and maple, growing from interlocking roots, appear like a single tree.

Along the heights of Forest Hill, groves of old oaks cast their shadows on the lawn.

9

*Over the deep ravine, through which a boulevard now runs,
a footbridge connects the two halves of Forest Hill.*

*Constructed of bluestone quarried
on the property, these simple
and graceful arches enhance
the sylvan quality of the Park.*

10

From the seven bridges that cross Dugway Brook, walkers may look down on its pools and curious shelving bed.

Built of the same stone and in the same spirit, the new footbridge spans Forest Hill Boulevard.

CLEVELAND'S CULTURAL GARDENS, a short distance from Forest Hill, are the spontaneous expression of a city of garden lovers. Gift inspired gift: in 1897 the senior Rockefeller gave lands and funds to complete a park along Doan Brook; in 1916, beginning with Clevelanders of English descent and their Shakespeare Garden, groups of various national lineages were inspired to create, along Doan Brook, gardens traditional to their motherlands, and to dedicate them to their greatest poets, musicians and philosophers. Nineteen gardens, in a chain extending a mile long, have now been dedicated: "In America, peace, understanding, amity and cooperation among the peoples of all nations."

In the Hungarian Garden, as in the others, steps and walks lead to gardens of different native styles.

*To the Shakespeare Garden, actors, poets
and dramatists have brought ivy, yew, a mulberry
from New Place, roses from Verona and
". . . daffodils that come before the swallow dares,
And take the winds of March with beauty."*

*In the Hebrew Garden one of the walks,
which radiate from the central fountain to form
the Star of David, leads to the Poets' Circle.*

*Goethe and Schiller dominate the German Garden; lindens and a hundred
other trees and shrubs have been brought from old Germany.*

13

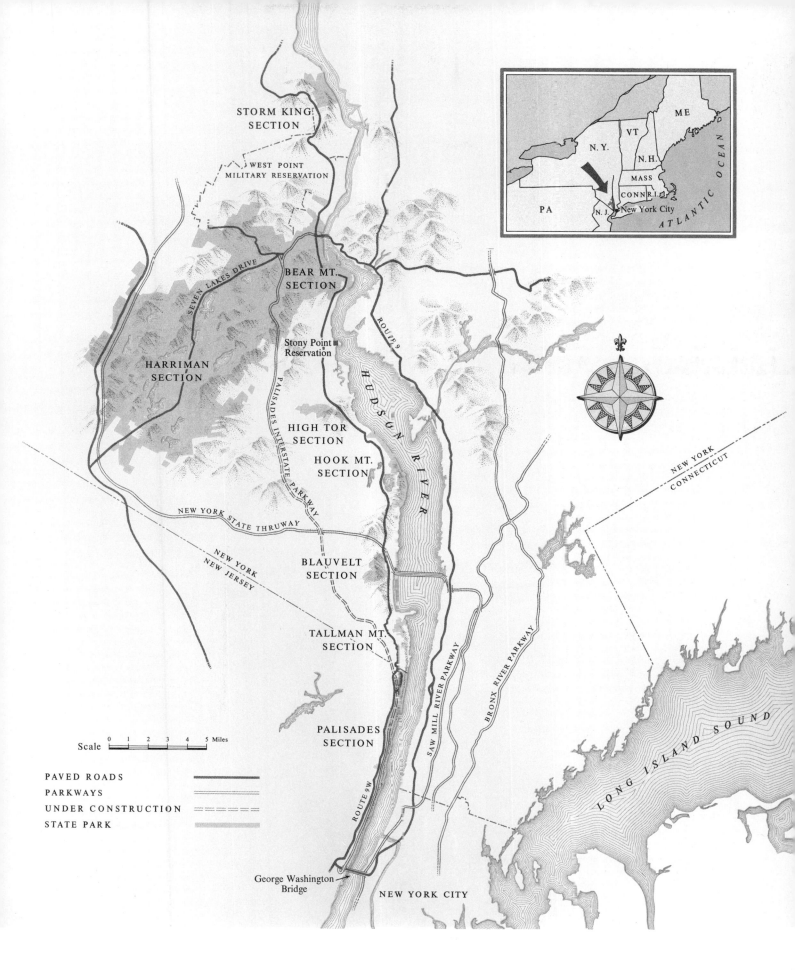

STORM KING
SECTION

WEST POINT
MILITARY RESERVATION

SEVEN LAKES DRIVE

BEAR MT.
SECTION

Stony Point
Reservation

HARRIMAN
SECTION

ROUTE 9

HUDSON RIVER

PALISADES INTERSTATE PARKWAY

HIGH TOR
SECTION

HOOK MT.
SECTION

NEW YORK STATE THRUWAY

NEW YORK
NEW JERSEY

BLAUVELT
SECTION

TALLMAN MT.
SECTION

PALISADES
SECTION

SAW MILL RIVER PARKWAY

BRONX RIVER PARKWAY

NEW YORK
CONNECTICUT

LONG ISLAND SOUND

Scale 0 1 2 3 4 5 Miles

PAVED ROADS
PARKWAYS
UNDER CONSTRUCTION
STATE PARK

ROUTE 9W

George Washington
Bridge

NEW YORK CITY

ME

N. Y.

VT

N.H.

MASS

CONN R.I.

PA

N. J. New York City

ATLANTIC OCEAN

THE PALISADES

THE HUDSON, springing from a lake high in the Adirondacks, is a tidal river, the salt water of the Atlantic flooding it for miles upstream. When Henry Hudson explored it in 1609, he found its shores "as pleasant a land as one can tread upon." On the western bank of the lower Hudson is a columnar wall thirty miles long. These tall prisms of traprock were early named "The Palisades." Below them, across the river, Manhattan appears and narrows like an arrowhead, and the Hudson widens into New York Bay.

On the east bank, settlements became cities. Along the west, only ferry landings and a few villages broke the cliffs when quarrymen found them ideal for crushed stone for concrete. Blasting resounded across the Hudson as headlands men had loved for centuries began to crumble. During the 1890's shocked citizens rallied on both sides of the river. In 1900 the legislatures of New York and New Jersey set up a permanent Interstate Park Commission. To save the Palisades, state cooperated with state, clubs and societies pooled efforts, individuals combined energies and funds; and the cliffside quarries were finally bought — to be stopped forever. George W. Perkins, President of the New York Commission for twenty years, inspired great gifts — three-quarters of a million from J. Pierpont Morgan; ten thousand acres of the Hudson Highlands, together with a million dollars toward purchasing Bear Mountain, from Mrs. E. H. Harriman; and more than three million dollars over the years from John D. Rockefeller, Sr., The Rockefeller Foundation, and the Laura Spelman Rockefeller Memorial.

By the 1920's the Palisades from top brink to shoreline belonged to the peoples of two states. But the skyline was still liable to exploitation. Anonymously, piece by piece, John D. Rockefeller, Jr., began buying land. Visiting the area repeatedly, he studied the terrain and made specific suggestions for the building of the Parkway. In 1935 he gave to the Interstate Park Commission some seven hundred acres, "to preserve the land lying along the top of the Palisades from any use inconsistent with your ownership and protection of the Palisades themselves."

The Palisades of the Hudson.

Rimming the Palisades, curving into forest, looking down from headlands on the Hudson, a parkway, when completed, will run from the George Washington Bridge to Bear Mountain.

18

At the first quarry bought, blasting stopped on Christmas Eve, 1900. But, day and night, blasting continued farther up the Hudson.

Not until the 1920's were the last quarriers stopped from grinding the Palisades to gravel and loading it onto barges to float downriver for the towers and pavements of Manhattan. Today the quarry floors are picnic grounds; pleasure boats tie up below.

AS THE PALISADES were sheared off, the towers of Manhattan rose. Demand for rock from the quarries — originally used for ballast and later, during the cobblestone era, for Belgian block pavement — became greater and greater, not only for the new skyscrapers but for the new macadamized and concrete streets of the city. Blasting and stone-crushing operations spread northward up the river, from Edgewater, across from Manhattan, past the New Jersey-New York state line, to Nyack and beyond. And the great, majestic cliffs, cut back by the stone-crushers, were disappearing in the dusts of man-made earthquakes of dynamite.

Skyscrapers, mushrooming in American cities by the early 1900's, consumed tons of crushed stone.

Early cars toiled up the few steep old roads winding up the Palisades.

Yearly, more cars ventured where none had been seen before: in 1916, 2,150 cars went to Bear Mountain; and by 1924 the number had increased to 1,159,000.

AS NEW AREAS UPRIVER were added to the Interstate Park — Storm King, Bear Mountain, Hook Mountain, Tallman Mountain, the Revolutionary battlefield at Stony Point, High Tor, Little Tor — the excursion boats already on the river could not carry all the crowds eager to see them. Through a gift from the Laura Spelman Rockefeller Memorial, two steamers were purchased by the Commission to carry park visitors. At park after park, the crowds grew. New trails, picnic groves, camping grounds and scenic drives were needed. Legislatures voted funds, citizens subscribed to bond issues, and the original donors and their descendants — four of whom, George W. Perkins, Jr., Laurance S. Rockefeller, and W. Averell and E. Roland Harriman, have served as Commissioners — continued to act whenever a place or an idea was in jeopardy. To help people from the cities understand what was around them, the American Museum of Natural History lent its staffs; and through another gift from the Laura Spelman Rockefeller Memorial, trails were made along which visitors could walk into wooded areas.

Steamships carried millions of visitors every year
from New York City up the Hudson to Bear Mountain.

Along the top of the Palisades, the Interstate Parkway flows smoothly— now among trees, now out beside the precipice.

Up toward Bear Mountain, the Parkway sweeps through rugged highlands.

From boat basin and parkway, trails lead off, beside the river, along the rim, up the cliffs.

A ROAD UNCLUTTERED, a road uninterrupted by signs, cities, traffic intersections, and unimpeded by opposing traffic — such a road is a release and a delight. The purpose of a scenic highway is to make driving a pleasure — to stop occasionally at overlooks to contemplate the broad views of valleys, rivers and hills. To such scenes, parkways in a motor age serve as introduction. The Palisades Interstate Parkway is an outstanding example of how individuals and governments can cooperate in joint efforts to preserve our natural heritage and to insure the wonders of our rich and varied land for future generations.

At Greenbrook Falls the sounds of the steeply cascading waters mingle with the songs of birds in a natural bird sanctuary.

To move out from the shore, across the Hudson, is to see the Palisades rise to their full height.

PLANS FOR THE FIRST MILE of the Palisades Parkway were brought to Mr. Rockefeller, Jr., who was anxious that the road not disturb the natural beauty of the heights. Inquiring the scale, he took out a carpenter's rule and began measuring the distances. The road, he felt, was too far from the rim; people should be able to look down as well as across. The engineers explained that where talus slopes buttressed the Palisades, they were safe; on steep cliff faces, a road too close would hasten the age-long fracturing. From this necessity sprang the idea of overlooks, which gathered trailheads and picnic groves around them.

A parkway is not a through-way but an invitation to linger at overlooks to view the scenery.

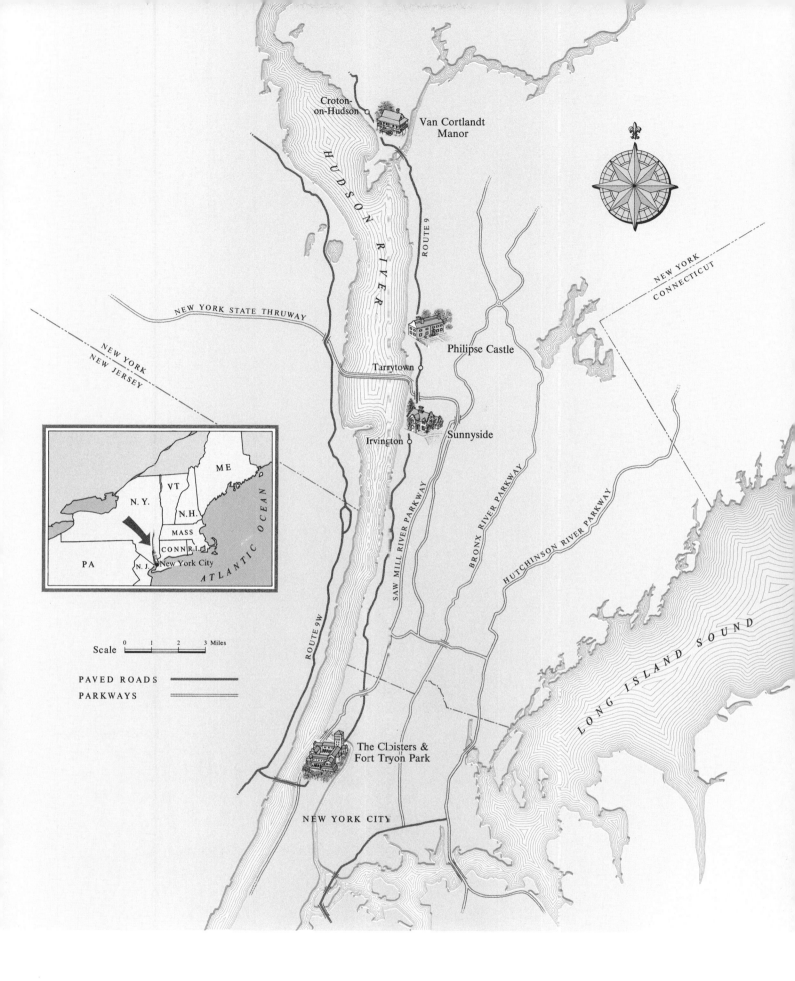

THE HUDSON VALLEY

THE EAST BANK OF THE HUDSON for nearly four centuries has played a significant role in American life and history. Up the valley of the Hudson, the Dutch founded towns, trading posts, vast estates and family dynasties of leaders. Long after the American Revolution, their influence persisted. Transformed by the pen of Washington Irving, they became legend. As a boy, Mr. Rockefeller, Jr., explored the Hudson and pored over Irving's *Sketch Book;* as a man — while his interests reached out through science, education and art across the world and into both past and future — he went on thinking and planning as a citizen of New York and a neighbor at Pocantico.

To New York City he gave Fort Tryon Park, commanding magnificent views of the Hudson. When he first offered it to the City in 1917, Mr. Rockefeller said, "All my life I have thought what a fine park this land would make." Nearby, the sculptor George Grey Barnard exhibited his collection of medieval sculpture and architecture, including sections of ruined French monasteries. In 1925 the Metropolitan Museum of Art, through a gift from Mr. Rockefeller, purchased this collection, known as the Cloisters, and re-opened it in 1926. When the City accepted Fort Tryon Park in 1930, four acres were reserved for a new building for The Cloisters, which was opened in 1938.

Up the Hudson, Mr. Rockefeller aided the Historical Society of the Tarrytowns to preserve Philipse Castle, a unique museum of early Dutch life in America. Through another gift, Irving's "elegant little snuggery," Sunnyside, was restored to reflect once more its owner's personality and interests. Another historic house, Van Cortlandt Manor — an outpost converted in 1688 into a dwelling where the Van Cortlandts lived until 1940 — was purchased in 1953 by Mr. Rockefeller, who undertook the difficult job of restoration.

In all this, as Malcolm Vaughan, editor of the *American Collector,* said, Mr. Rockefeller "is always doing something that others have overlooked; or, to state the circumstances more precisely: in the sphere of art and cultural history, he increasingly sets himself the mission of doing what otherwise might never be undertaken."

The Cloisters at Fort Tryon Park.

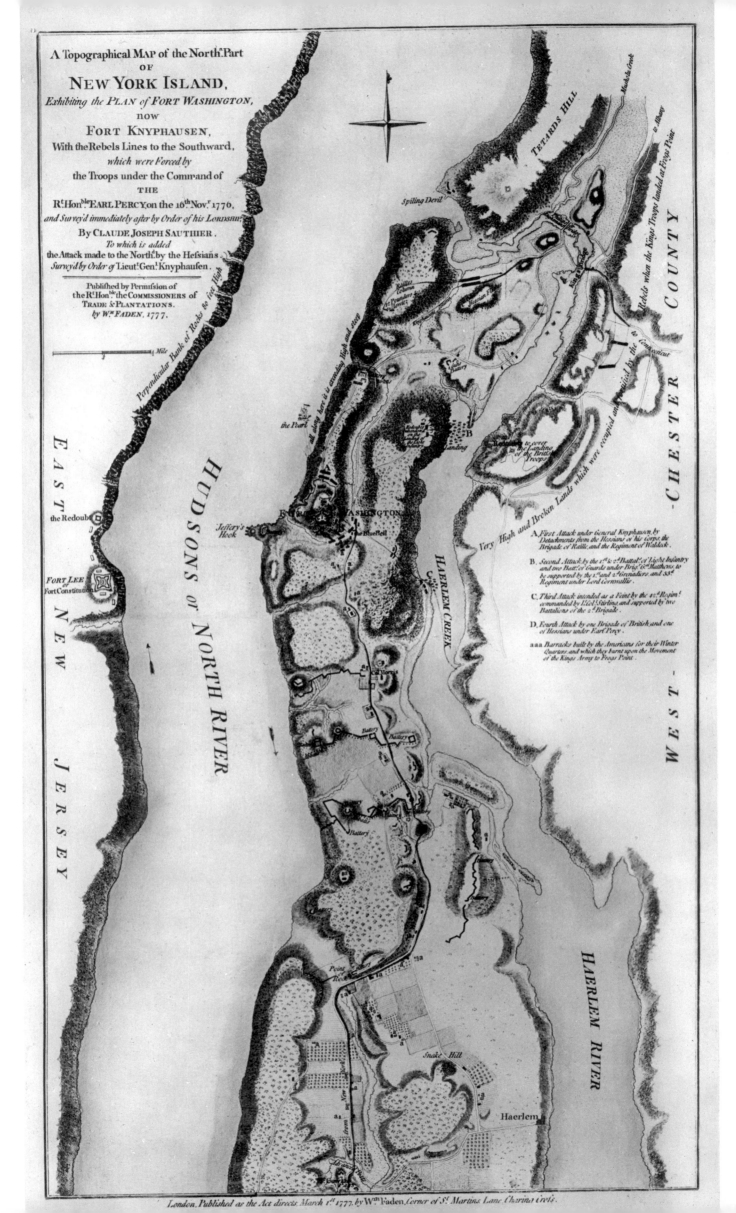

A Topographical MAP of the North Part
OF
NEW YORK ISLAND,
Exhibiting the PLAN of FORT WASHINGTON,
now
FORT KNYPHAUSEN,
With the Rebels Lines to the Southward,
which were Forced by
the Troops under the Command of
THE
R.t Hon.ble EARL PERCY, on the 16.th Nov.r 1776,
and Survey'd immediately after by Order of his Lordship.
By CLAUDE JOSEPH SAUTHIER.
To which is added
the Attack made to the North by the Hessians.
Survey'd by Order of Lieut.t Gen.l Knyphausen.

Published by Permission of
the R.t Hon.ble the COMMISSIONERS of
TRADE & PLANTATIONS.
by W.m FADEN. 1777.

¼ Mile

EAST

NEW JERSEY

the Redoubt

FORT LEE
or
Fort Constitution

Perpendicular Bank of Rocks &c 160 High

HUDSONS or NORTH RIVER

Jeffery's Hook

all along here is exceeding High and steep

the Pearl

FORT WASHINGTON
the Bluebell

Spiling Devil

TETARDS HILL

Mockata Creek

to Albany

King's Bridge

Hessian Fort

Rebels when the Kings Troops landed at Frogs Point

CHESTER COUNTY

WEST

Redoubt to cover the Landing of the British Troops

B

Very High and Broken Lands which were escaped and possessed by the Connecticut

HAERLEM CREEK

C

A. *First Attack under General Knyphausen, by
Detachments from the Hessians of his Corps, the
Brigade of Raille, and the Regiment of Waldeck.*

B. *Second Attack by the 1.st & 2.d Battal.s of Light Infantry
and two Battl.s of Guards under Brig.r Gen.l Matthews, to
be supported by the 1.st and 2.d Grenadiers, and 33.d
Regiment under Lord Cornwallis.*

C. *Third Attack intended as a Feint by the 42.d Regim.t
commanded by Lt. Col. Stirling, and supported by two
Battalions of the 2.d Brigade.*

D. *Fourth Attack by one Brigade of British and one
of Hessians under Earl Percy.*

aaa *Barracks built by the Americans for their Winter
Quarters, and which they burnt upon the Movement
of the Kings Army to Frogs Point.*

Col. Norris

Battery

Battery

Battery

Point
Rock

Snake Hill

HAERLEM RIVER

Haerlem

ON NOVEMBER 16, 1776, the steep height then called Forest Hill was the northern outpost of Fort Washington. Raw American colonials in its redoubts were shelled by the British frigate *Pearl* below in the Hudson, cannonaded from the heights across the Harlem, stormed by Hessians, Highlanders and redcoats from all sides. Although hopelessly outnumbered, the Americans fired down through the bare trees, forcing the enemy, as one of them reported, "to creep along the rocks, one man falling down alive, another shot or dead . . . to drag ourselves by the birch tree bushes up the height when we really could not stand." Washington, watching from Fort Lee, is said to have wept as his troops finally lost the unequal combat.

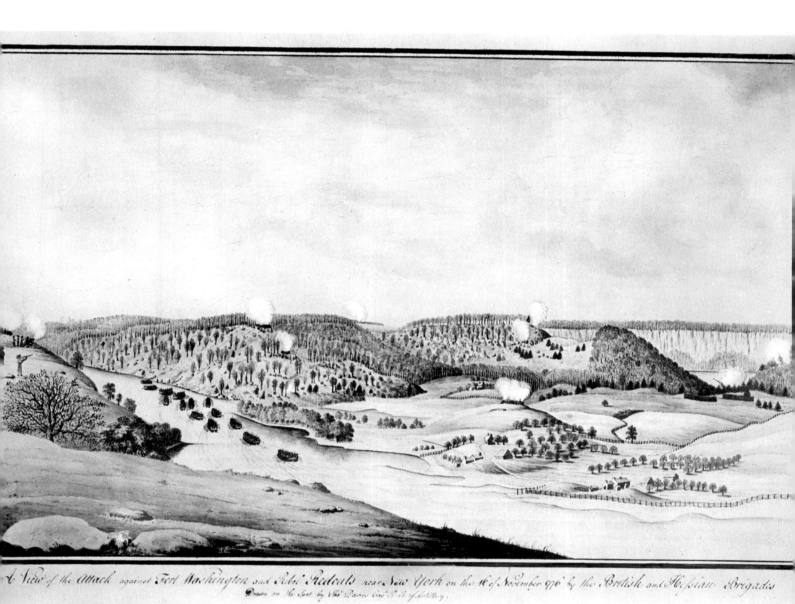

Capturing Forest Hill after fierce resistance, the British renamed it after Royal Governor Tryon.

The walks, drives and bridges of Fort Tryon Park lead to The Cloisters,
whose hilltop setting recalls medieval abbeys in Europe.

THE CLOISTERS were designed around their contents. A model was constructed
first at Mr. Rockefeller's suggestion and helped him to point out the need he had
foreseen for alterations in the original plans. He followed the construction work
closely, while the chapter house from Pontaut and the cloisters from Cuxa, Saint-
Guilhem, Bonnefont and Trie were set in masonry of their style — often hewn from
the original quarries. Of The Cloisters' collection of chalices, tapestries, sculpture,
Mr. Rockefeller gave over ninety per cent, some of which had been collected by him
in earlier years. Set about with ramparts and buttresses, dominated by a tower like
that at Cuxa, graced with fountains, gardens and, at certain hours, medieval music,
The Cloisters have attracted more than seven million visitors.

King Arthur was part of the fourteenth-century Nine Heroes tapestries. Mr. Rockefeller consulted with museum experts on such details as the effect of sunlight on the tapestries and the proper setting for their display.

The seven tapestries of the Hunt of the Unicorn, woven for the marriage of Anne of Brittany and Louis XII, were imported by Mr. Rockefeller from France to hang originally in his own home.

35

From farms and villages,
sculptor Barnard rescued
the bold capitals and serene arches
of the Cuxa cloister.

In the Trie cloister, delicate arcades
enclose a fountain surmounted by a cross
and set in a garden of yews and ivy.

Through such cloisters as Bonnefont, saints,
monks and poets paced in meditation.

Heraldic symbols were
rendered in stained glass.
This window bears the arms
of Emperor Maximilian.

All new masonry, as in this archway,
follows simple, authentic styles.

Many fragments, such as
this fifteenth-century doorway
and the fireplace beyond,
have been built into the walls.

Abbots, such as the one here portrayed in Benedictine habit, governed the monasteries. They held office for life.

Majestic and gentle, this Virgin once adorned the thirteenth-century choir screen of Strasbourg Cathedral.

In the Chalice of Antioch, openwork of gilded silver holds the simple cup once thought to be the Holy Grail.

UP THE HUDSON, twenty-five miles from New York, is Washington Irving's land of Sleepy Hollow. This includes his own gabled house, Sunnyside, and also part of the Rockefeller family estate at Pocantico. Sunnyside, described by Irving as "a little old fashioned stone mansion, all made up of gable ends, and as full of angles and corners as an old cocked hat," was his delight. From diplomatic service abroad, Irving came back rejoicing to the countryside he had immortalized as Sleepy Hollow, whose memorable characters like Ichabod Crane have been familiar to Mr. Rockefeller since childhood.

Sunnyside was bought by Irving in 1835. It was acquired for preservation in 1945, and two years were needed for the painstaking restoration.

The study where Irving wrote the "Life of Washington" has been restored from descriptions in old letters and contemporary drawings.

One of the most beloved men of his time,
Irving enjoyed entertaining.
Prince Louis Napoleon, President Martin
Van Buren, poet William Cullen Bryant
are among the famous men who dined here.

Evenings of music delighted Irving —
good voices, a harp, a niece playing the spinet
and himself with a flute.
"Our parties always end with a dance."

Cookery in Irving's time
was still done at the open hearth,
though stoves were coming in.

At Philipse Castle, the old well, the slave hut, the smokehouse, a barn complete with gear, the mill and the trading post have been restored.

PHILIPSE CASTLE was built by Frederick Philipse in 1683 as solid as a fortress. Guns could be fired through gunports in its foundations; a secret passage led up to the attic. The Hudson valley then was wilderness, yet Philipse built out into the Tappan Zee a dock where his own ships from Hong Kong or Amsterdam could tie up. Beside the Pocantico River, he built a mill and trading post, set a dam across the stream and a footbridge above it. The manor house was to be razed in 1940, when Mr. Rockefeller made possible its preservation and restoration. By 1943 it again looked as it had in the seventeenth and eighteenth centuries.

Confiscated after the Revolution, the Castle was bought by Gerard Beekman, who added the wooden wing in 1785.

*Down a ramp into the cellar,
cattle were driven when pirate ships
came up the river or
raiding Indians attacked.*

THE DUTCH ON THE HUDSON lived in cheerful and efficient comfort. Rooms were small and snug, with wide shallow hearths to warm them. White sand, patterned and frequently renewed, lay on floors trampled by muddy feet. A year's supply of food was stored in the cellar, where slaves polished brass and copper, churned butter, pressed cheese, and cooked for themselves and the family upstairs. On looms in the attic, common stuffs were woven. From Europe and the Orient the Dutch imported fine fabrics, china and furniture. Life was warm, gracious, prosperous.

*In the parlor stands
a painted kas (chest) from
Zaandam; a Turkish carpet
covers the table.*

The manor at Croton-on-Hudson was built before 1686, when it was first mentioned in a recorded deed.

An ancient column of the manor was well preserved at top but had to be restored at bottom.

VAN CORTLANDT MANOR, a seventeenth-century trading post and hunting lodge, was bought in 1688 by Stephanus Van Cortlandt, a merchant and landowner who was the first native-born mayor of New York. It was first used as a permanent residence in 1749 by the third proprietor, Pierre Van Cortlandt, who enlarged the house and added double verandas. The house was for two centuries thereafter the home of Van Cortlandts. The last Van Cortlandt resident died in 1940. Mr. Rockefeller in 1953 bought the house described by architectural historians as "one of the most important landmarks of the nation," so that "it would not be destroyed or turned into a business property." After layer upon layer of post-eighteenth-century repairs and embellishments were removed, and thousands of family papers and historic documents were studied for information about the buildings on the property, the work of restoring the Manor House and its surroundings began. Mr. Rockefeller made biweekly visits to review the problems of the restoration as they came up in the actual work of the architects and carpenters.

PART TWO: NATIONAL PARKS

EASTERN BAY

FRENCHMAN BAY

WESTERN BAY

SOMES SOUND

MOUNT DESERT ISLAND

Eagle Lake

The Bubbles

Echo Lake

Long Pond

Jordan Pond

Pemetic Mt.

Cadillac Mt.

Bar Harbor

Park Headquarters

Schoodic Head

SCHOODIC PENINSULA

Sand Beach

Great Head

Thunder Hole

Otter Cliffs

Seal Harbor

Northeast Harbor

Southwest Harbor

Islesford Historical Museum

BLUE HILL BAY

UNION RIVER BAY

ATLANTIC OCEAN

ME

VT

N. Y.

N. H.

MASS

Boston

ATLANTIC OCEAN

Scale 0 ½ 1 2 Miles

MAIN ROADS

SECONDARY ROADS

CARRIAGE ROADS

CAMPGROUNDS

PARK ENTRANCES

NATIONAL PARK

ACADIA

ACADIA, first National Park established east of the Mississippi, is dominated by the granite dome of Mount Cadillac, at whose fifteen-hundred-foot crest the rising sun first touches the United States. Here, a full-circle view surrounds the visitor. A hundred miles to the north rises Mount Katahdin. One hundred and fifty miles to the west are the White Mountains of New Hampshire. Below, down through woodlands, past shimmering lakes, to the little villages rimming its coves and harbors, Mount Desert Island falls to the sea. Split like a lobster claw by Somes Sound, the Island's sixty-mile periphery is as intricate as a fern frond. East and south, the shining ocean, sprinkled with islands, stretches away to the horizon.

For nearly five centuries, beginning with the mariners of the 1500's, the hills of Acadia have been a familiar sight to Atlantic voyagers. To thousands of people its diversified scenery has been one of the great natural beauties of the world. By the 1870's, as the names of Island communities — Bar Harbor, Northeast Harbor, Seal Harbor — became world famous, the Island began to attract visitors in such volume that its natural beauties were threatened with destruction by hastily improvised accommodations. In 1901 President Charles W. Eliot of Harvard, and George B. Dorr, summer residents, began to solicit gifts of land and money from other residents to save the Island. These lands, given to the United States in 1916, eventually became the first National Park to be composed entirely of gifts from individuals. Mr. Rockefeller, Jr., donated 2,700 acres to round out the Park from Frenchman Bay on the north to the Atlantic on the south. In 1917 he conceived an idea to make the area more than a preserve; he originated plans sent to the Secretary of the Interior, offering to build and maintain a road system to open up the lovely vistas of Acadia to visitors. Pursuing an old enthusiasm, he spent hours with surveyors and engineers in designing and constructing some sixty miles of roadways and bridges. In general, the purpose of his gifts to Acadia through the years was to make more accessible to visitors what he regarded "as one of the greatest views in the world."

The view from Mount Cadillac.

49

THIRD-LARGEST ISLAND of the continental coast of the United States, Mount Desert has an unequaled variety of scenery: eighteen mountains of the Appalachian chain, twenty-six lakes and ponds, five bays and harbors, countless streams, scores of massive coastal rock formations. From one spot in the Acadia National Park, a range of mountains, a placid lake, an archipelago and the open ocean are visible at once. Here, where the northern and temperate zones meet, is an extraordinary diversity of plant life, ranging from two to three hundred species and including both the Arctic Labrador tea and twenty varieties of orchids.

Erratic boulders from the mainland were left precariously perched on Acadia slopes by the glacier.

50

The gentle domes of Acadia's mountains were shaped by the last Ice Age, which also scooped out basins for ponds.

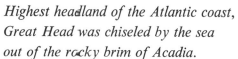

Highest headland of the Atlantic coast, Great Head was chiseled by the sea out of the rocky brim of Acadia.

At high tide the spray of the pounding surf sometimes rises to sixty feet at Thunder Hole.

The French geographer-explorer, de Champlain, impressed by the barren tops of the Island's summits, called it "Island of the Desert Mountains."

CLAIMING FOR FRANCE the land he "baptized Acadia for the beauty of its trees," the voyager, Verrazzano, charted the coast for Francis I in 1524. Eighty years later, Samuel de Champlain stopped at Bar Harbor to repair a ship "stove on a rock" and noted "an island four or five leagues long, high and notched in places, so that from the sea it gives the appearance of a range of seven or eight mountains. The slopes are covered with pines, firs and birches. The summits are all bare and rocky." In 1613 a little company of French Jesuits and settlers landed at Mount Desert when a dense fog stopped their ship from sailing on to Penobscot. Urged by the Indians to stay, they raised their cross beside Somes Sound and founded there the mission colony of St. Sauveur. Six months later they were saving souls and raising crops when Captain Samuel Argall sailed up from the English colony of Jamestown in Virginia to expel the French settlers from the English-claimed lands. But by 1688 the Island was again in French possession, and Louis XIV gave it in feudal fief to the Sieur de la Mothe Cadillac, who brought his bride there. The British won it back again in 1713 and kept it until the American Revolution.

Somes Sound was the site of an early French mission, which converted friendly Indians to Christianity.

The cliffs of Acadia enchanted early voyagers, who found the rocky heights "marvellous to behold."

Bar Harbor and the surrounding lands became a tourist mecca in the late 1800's, bringing a flood of exploiters.

NINETEENTH-CENTURY RESORTS boomed on Mount Desert. Vacationists, streaming in from eastern cities, crowded the villages, the new rough hotels, and even tents pitched in any spot available. Steamship lines were established in 1868, followed rapidly by exploiters determined to make the most of the Island's newly discovered popularity. Introduction of the portable sawmill also threatened the Island's trees. To preserve the woodlands, the remarkably varied wildlife, the magnificent views, alert citizens formed a group to acquire and redeem most of the primitive terrain and preserve it. First held as a public trust, the land was accepted by the United States as Sieur de Monts National Monument in 1916, became Lafayette National Park in 1919, and had its name changed to Acadia in 1929.

*A boxlike hotel was perched atop
Cadillac Mountain to accommodate the visitors
of the 1880's, with complete disregard
for the natural beauty of the
most prominent crest of the Island.*

*A path was chopped up the mountainside for a cog railroad,
whose proprietor dynamited a competing carriage road.*

A PARK PERFECTED, stretching from Frenchman Bay to the ocean itself, with roadways opening up its vistas and making its heights accessible to visitors, was the ambition of John D. Rockefeller, Jr. Quietly buying up land to supplement the areas already given the Park, he was also thinking of how the roads could be threaded through the hills to blend with the natural features of the landscape and leave no scars. First working out on paper the curves, bridges and overpasses, and then vigilantly following construction on the spot, Mr. Rockefeller worked closely with the engineers, hiring in seasons when work was scarce on the Island and relaxing the pace when other jobs were plentiful. As each unit was completed, it was deeded to the Government as a gift from Mr. Rockefeller.

A few feet from the roadways and trails are vantage points for such remarkable views as Echo Lake.

*Bridges and overpasses were designed to Mr. Rockefeller's specifications
to permit uninterrupted drives through the Park.*

*Conceived when motor cars were still barred from the Island
and there were only foot trails in the Park,
the roads were built for leisurely rides in carriages.*

For the era of the motor car, a scenic ocean drive around the rim of the Park was begun in the 1920's.

The roads were carefully designed
to blend gently into
the Acadia landscape.

*The rustic grace of old country roads
was achieved by sensitive regard
for surroundings in laying out the roads.*

The Ocean Drive winds around a magnificent beach.

59

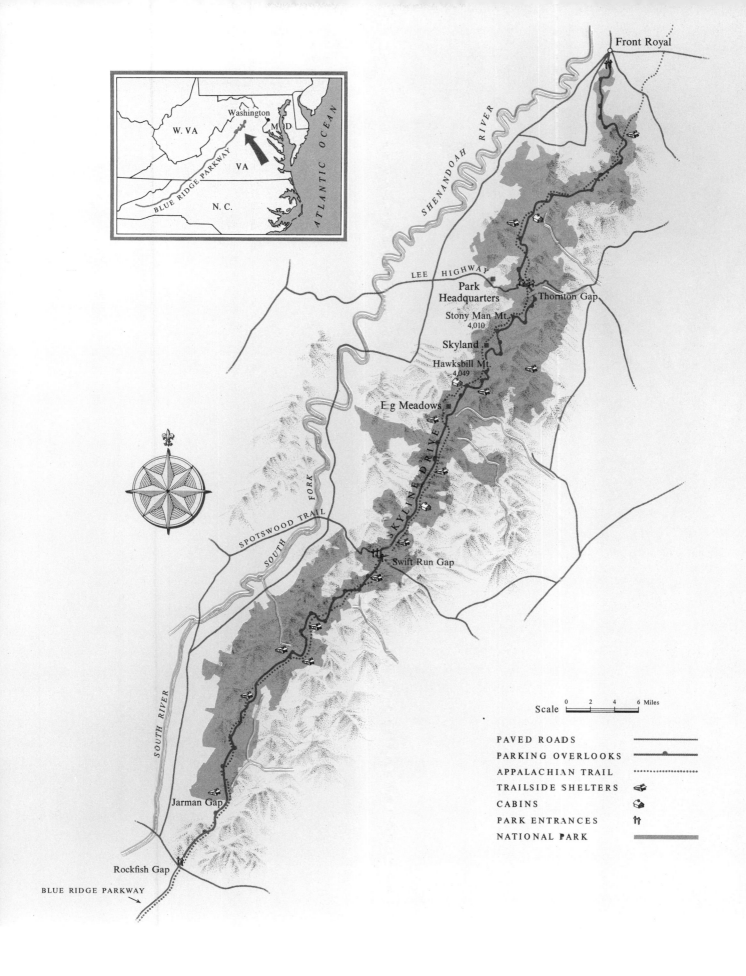

Front Royal

SHENANDOAH RIVER

LEE HIGHWAY

Park
Headquarters

Thornton Gap

Stony Man Mt.
4,010

Skyland

Hawksbill Mt.
4,049

E g Meadows

SKYLINE DRIVE

SPOTSWOOD TRAIL

SOUTH FORK

Swift Run Gap

SOUTH RIVER

Jarman Gap

Rockfish Gap

BLUE RIDGE PARKWAY

Washington

W. VA

VA

MD

ATLANTIC OCEAN

BLUE RIDGE PARKWAY

N. C.

Scale

0   2   4   6 Miles

PAVED ROADS
PARKING OVERLOOKS
APPALACHIAN TRAIL
TRAILSIDE SHELTERS
CABINS
PARK ENTRANCES
NATIONAL PARK

SHENANDOAH

SHENANDOAH — "Daughter of the Stars" in an Indian tongue — is one of the most luxuriant of all the National Parks. Deep in Virginia's Blue Ridge Mountains, part of the same Appalachian range that stretches to the Acadian hills, the Park's 193,480 acres are ninety-five per cent rich and varied forests, five per cent lovely, open meadows. Sixty mountain peaks, ranging from 2,000 to 4,000 feet, reach up to blend their gentle summits with the billows of blue haze that give the mountains their name.

Thought by geologists to be the oldest land on the face of the earth (since the granite Blue Ridge has resisted erosion throughout the ages), Shenandoah is one of the youngest of the National Parks. With Great Smoky, Shenandoah was first approved by Congress in 1926, when Mount Desert had the only National Park east of the Mississippi. Actual establishment of the Park, however, depended upon the people of Virginia acquiring the land and deeding it to the Federal Government. Unlike the western Parks, these were not public lands but privately owned and, in many cases, in one family's possession since colonial times. Virginians raised $1,200,000 to make their beautiful highlands a gift to the American people. Other public-spirited citizens also participated in making the gift possible. John D. Rockefeller, Jr., was among the contributors.

Primarily scenic in its appeal, irresistible alike to the forty million who live within a day's ride and to those who cross the continent to see its transcendent colors, Shenandoah offers in its Skyline Drive a remarkable vantage point for viewing the panoramas of the Shenandoah Valley to the west and the lowlands of the Piedmont Plateau to the east. For over a hundred miles, the Skyline Drive stretches, like a ribbon down a bright tapestry, along the ridge. At Rockfish Gap, Skyline merges into Blue Ridge Parkway. Off the Parkway at Linville Falls, the Linville River plunges 150 feet, and then tumbles 1,200 feet lower down a twelve-mile gorge. When the setting of the sparkling falls was threatened by the lumbering of the surrounding hemlocks, Mr. Rockefeller gave the funds to preserve "that beautiful area."

The Shenandoah Valley.

*Frequent overlooks make it possible
for drivers along Blue Ridge
Parkway to stop, look at the views
and learn more about
the mountains and valleys.*

Between Roanoke and the Peaks of Otter the fog settles low over the Jefferson National Forest.

Stony Man Mountain, second-highest peak in the Park, looks down over the Shenandoah Valley.

SKYLINE DRIVE runs from 600 to 3,630 feet above sea level as it winds along the mountain tops down the full length of the Shenandoah National Park. In precolonial times, an Indian trail ran along this same ridge, and by the time of the Revolution, the striking beauty of Shenandoah was already familiar to Americans. "Equal to the promised land in fertility," wrote Washington Irving of the Valley, "and far superior to it for beauty." The nine years of labor that went into the construction of the Drive forged the first link in a 700-mile grand scenic highway, extending from Front Royal, eighty miles southwest of Washington, to the heart of the Tennessee Smokies. Blue Ridge Parkway, connecting Shenandoah with Great Smoky, winds nearly 500 miles to the southwest, still following the crests of the Appalachians that make up the superbly arboreal Southern Highlands with their wide, verdant valleys.

Camp sites are available to visitors at Big Meadows and Lewis Mountain.

At Hawksbill Shelter on the Appalachian Trail, hikers check their equipment with a National Park naturalist. The Trail, passing through Shenandoah, extends from Maine to Georgia.

Hundreds of unexpected trails lead off the Skyline Drive onto the mountainsides. Park rangers lead explorers on by-trips along the trails.

*From the terrace at Big Meadows Lodge,
a photographer studies
the panorama of Shenandoah Valley.*

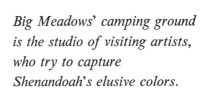

*Big Meadows' camping ground
is the studio of visiting artists,
who try to capture
Shenandoah's elusive colors.*

THE LEISURELY ENJOYMENT of Shenandoah's scenery lures over a million visitors a year to the Park. Painters and photographers, both amateur and professional, have taken back to their homes all over the nation their records and impressions of scenes unsurpassed for the loveliness of changing colors and the serenity of distant landscapes. Within easy access of the Blue Ridge Parkway are such more intimate scenes as waterfalls and, occasionally, buildings that had been standing on these lands long before they were part of the National Park system.

The old Mabry Mill on the Blue Ridge Parkway is still grinding flour.

Linville Falls delighted Mr. Rockefeller when he first saw it. Later he made possible adding the gorge to the Blue Ridge preserves.

69

LITTLE PIGEON

RIVER

Gatlinburg

Park Headquarters

Townsend

Ramsey Cascades

Mt. Guyot
6,621

Mt. Chapman
6,430

Mt. Le Conte
6,593

TENNESSEE

Newfound Gap

CADES
COVE

Clingmans Dome
6,643

NORTH CAROLINA

CHEROKEE
INDIAN
RESERVATION

BLUE RIDGE PARKWAY

PROPOSED

LAKE FONTANA

Scale 0 2 4 6 Miles

PAVED ROADS

SECONDARY ROADS

PARKING OVERLOOKS

APPALACHIAN TRAIL

CAMPGROUNDS

SHELTER CABINS

PIONEER STRUCTURES

NATIONAL PARK

GREAT SMOKY MOUNTAINS

GREAT SMOKY MOUNTAINS, linked to Shenandoah by Blue Ridge Parkway, are the highest peaks in the great Appalachian chain. For half its 71-mile length, the Great Smoky range towers over five thousand feet into a haze that deepens into smoke-like clouds. "This massive and high citadel," as the explorer Arnold Guyot called it, is forty per cent virgin forests. Within its 800 square miles are more species of native trees than in all 3,570,000 square miles of Europe. Vegetation is so varied that Park naturalists say that, in driving a single mile from its lowlands to its highlands, a visitor encounters the same range in flora he would meet during a thousand-mile drive from Georgia to New England. Here, in the hospitable climate of Tennessee and North Carolina, flowers blossom from February to December; and shrubs and bushes, a few feet high in other areas, grow to giant size in the rich soil.

Now the property of the American people, this highest National Park east of the Mississippi was preserved through the persistent faith of those who refused to be discouraged through all the delays and difficulties of acquiring funds to buy half a million acres from private owners. By 1926 the people and states of Tennessee and North Carolina had raised over a million dollars. In May, 1926, Congress authorized the establishment of the Park, if the necessary additional funds could be secured to buy the land. Again those who knew these flowering hills best were first to respond: North Carolina raised another $2,000,000, Tennessee another $1,500,000 — a total, by 1928, of some $5,000,000. But all efforts to raise more outside the region failed.

Long deeply interested in creating more parks convenient to the teeming population centers of the eastern part of the country, Mr. Rockefeller suggested that the Laura Spelman Rockefeller Memorial make a gift of $5,000,000 as a memorial to "the beautiful spirit of my mother." With this gift, matching funds already raised, the Park became a reality. Twenty-five years later, the Directors of the Great Smoky Mountains Conservation Association resolved that the "timely and far-sighted gift . . . will stand through the ages as a living memorial to a wonderful woman."

Great Smokies foliage.

Omnipresent, smoke-like mist
rises from the lowlands to ring
the Great Smokies' peaks
in wreaths of haze. Plentiful rains
leave the air almost constantly
moist and the ground damp.
Then, as the southern sun
warms the ground, a light fog
ascends the slopes,
hovers just below the summits.

Autumn is the driest season, converting the lush southern hills into perhaps the most variegated landscape in America.

A VAST NATURAL BOTANICAL GARDEN, Great Smoky has more than 1,400 species of flowering plants and shrubs, blooming from late winter until late autumn. Tulip trees grow until their trunks measure over seventeen feet in circumference; grapevines have stems five feet around; wild cherry trees have been recorded four feet in girth. The unbroken forest cover of the Great Smokies is primarily made up of hardwoods — some of them blazing red and golden in late October — oaks and maples, beech, poplar, hickory, birch, cherry, sycamore and scores of others. The wild flowers and shrubs, with their long blossoming season, include 50 different kinds of lily, 22 kinds of violet, many varieties of geranium, ladyslipper, columbine, magnolia, trillium. But dominating all are, in late June and July, the remarkable rhododendron; in May and June, the ubiquitous mountain laurel; and in June, the fiery flame azalea.

The sourwoods of the Smokies are noted for the brilliance of their autumn foliage. Native to the eastern United States, they grow all along the Allegheny Mountain ridge.

Early summer is the season of the mountain laurel, which grows so thick in the Smokies that animals sometimes are trapped in it.

77

FUR-BEARING ANIMALS of the Great Smokies include at least 52 species. One of the most common is the black bear, which has so intrigued tourists here and in other National Parks that it has become a kind of unofficial symbol of the Parks. Before 1923, when the movement to make the area a preserve began, wildlife was threatened with extinction by completely uncontrolled hunting. The Virginia white-tailed deer are returning, and the Park Service is restocking the area with other almost-vanished species.

National Park visitors love to watch the bears, but are warned not to molest, touch or feed them.

Black bears have adjusted themselves
to the inroads made on their old tramping
grounds. The Park Service advises
campers to hang their food supplies from
tree limbs, out of reach of the marauding bears.

Cubs are gregarious and curious,
but usually stay deep in the woods.

Some sections of the highway
are frequented by bears, which rangers
warn are dangerous when tempted by food.

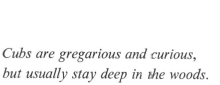

*Trails through the Great Smokies
take hikers into areas and
reveal to them views virtually unknown
— except to native mountaineers —
before the Park was opened.*

*Ramsey Cascades, largest of scores in the
Great Smokies, are reached on foot from Greenbrier.
Deep in a stand of virgin hardwoods,
the cascades are at an elevation of 4,750 feet.*

80

A wild-flower pilgrimage group studies a species which most of the enthusiasts are equipped to record in photographs.

From the Rockefeller Memorial at Newfound Gap, visitors look out at Clingman's Dome, highest peak in the Park. Overlooks and parking areas are indispensable features of scenic parks.

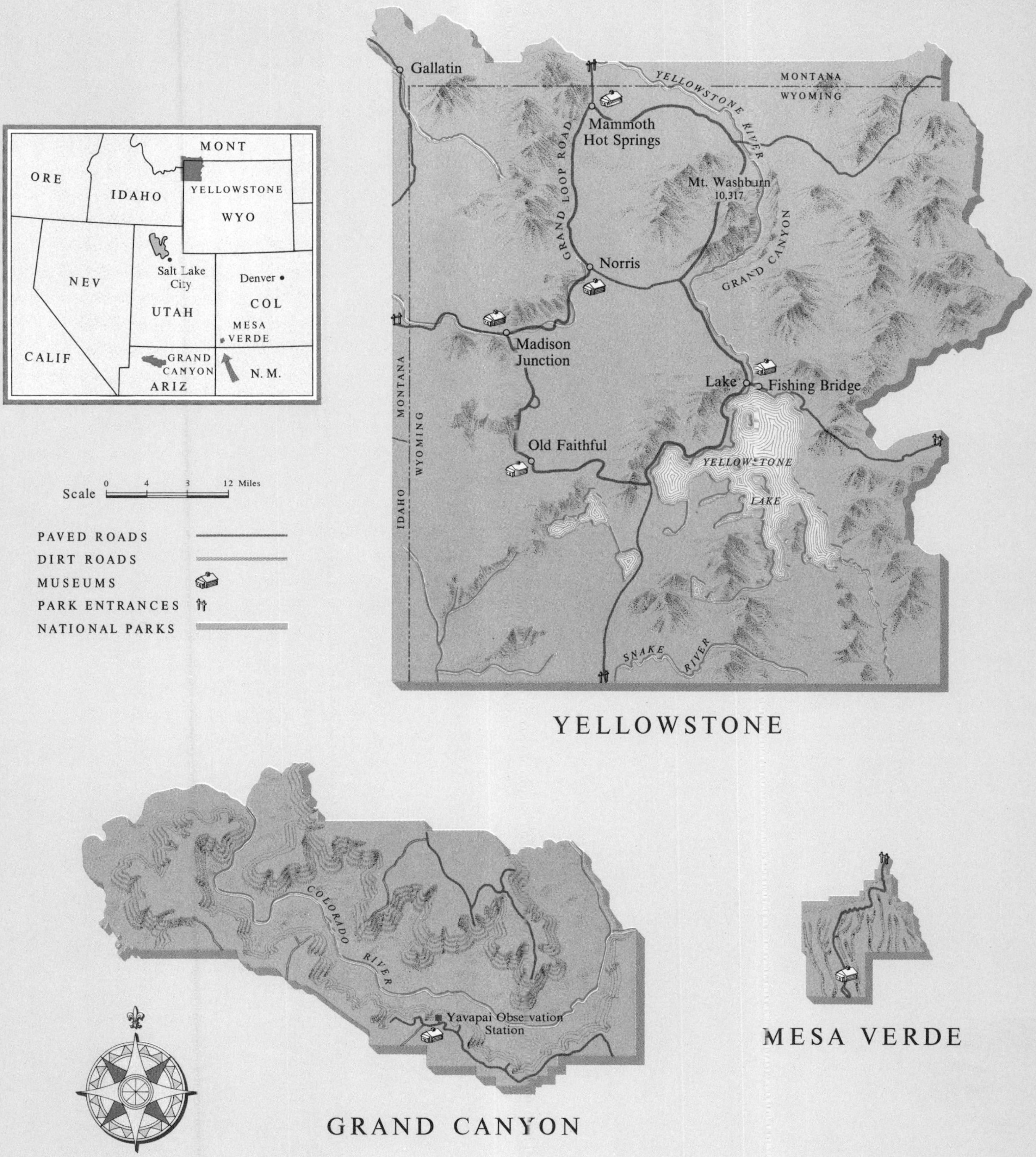
MONT
ORE
IDAHO
YELLOWSTONE
WYO
NEV
Salt Lake City
UTAH
Denver
COL
MESA VERDE
CALIF
GRAND CANYON
ARIZ
N. M.
Scale 0 4 8 12 Miles
PAVED ROADS
DIRT ROADS
MUSEUMS
PARK ENTRANCES
NATIONAL PARKS
Gallatin
YELLOWSTONE RIVER
MONTANA
WYOMING
Mammoth Hot Springs
GRAND LOOP ROAD
Mt. Washburn 10,317
GRAND CANYON
Norris
Madison Junction
Lake
Fishing Bridge
Old Faithful
YELLOWSTONE LAKE
IDAHO
SNAKE RIVER
YELLOWSTONE
COLORADO RIVER
Yavapai Observation Station
GRAND CANYON
MESA VERDE

MUSEUMS

A MUSEUM AT MESA VERDE, helping to explain the wonders of the Park to visitors, was developed following a tour through the western National Parks on which Mr. Rockefeller took his three oldest sons in 1924. Another result was the cleaning up of roadsides in Yellowstone. Both were pilot projects, undertaken to demonstrate their value to the nation. The National Park Service was then only eight years old. In 1915 Stephen T. Mather, philanthropist, accepted the challenge of Franklin K. Lane, Secretary of the Interior: "If you don't like the way the Parks are run, Steve, come down here and run them yourself." Mather thought setting up the Parks would take a year: it took the rest of his life. Magnificent areas had been acquired down the years, but regions equally spectacular still lay open to ruinous use. Some Parks had been run by the Army, some by other agencies. Roads were often bad, accommodations inadequate, natural wonders debased to side shows. Much had been accomplished — better roads, accommodations, a National Park Service of loyal and intelligent men — but only tentative beginnings of the interpretive program planned by Mather had been possible.

Among the Park Superintendents Mr. Rockefeller met on this trip were: Jesse Nusbaum, at Mesa Verde, who showed him how much was added by oral and visual interpretation on the spot; and Horace Albright, at Yellowstone, later Director of the National Park Service, with whom he was to consult on conservation projects for the next thirty years. The Park Service found Mr. Rockefeller, as Herbert Maier, architect of the museums, said, "a traveller with a highly intellectual curiosity. Whatever he saw prompted a stream of questions. Indeed, in the Parks, he was that ideal tourist we love to envision."

Whenever he arrived at a clear perception of what was needed, Mr. Rockefeller went to work. Since Congress failed to act on certain vital issues, he believed it was up to private initiative to prove their importance. Some pilot funds for the museums were provided by the Laura Spelman Rockefeller Memorial and by Mr. Rockefeller personally.

The ancient cliff houses of Mesa Verde.

85

Mr. Rockefeller, Superintendent Nusbaum recalled, spent hours at Cliff Palace,
"quietly contemplating this great ruin and its canyon terrain . . . Periodically he
would ask me some pertinent question . . . where they farmed, how
they farmed, the source of their water supply, their ways of life, ceremonials . . ."

MESA VERDE — a vast tableland twenty miles long and two thousand feet high, whose rimrocks command the horizon for more than a hundred miles, up through the Rockies and down across the desert — is honeycombed on its south side with deep canyons. Here, in long crannies and huge arching caves, stand hundreds of cliff dwellings abandoned two centuries before Columbus.

Up the steep road to the mesa top in 1924 came Mr. Rockefeller and his sons John 3rd, Nelson and Laurance. Superintendent Nusbaum led them to look down, from the porch of the temporary log cabin museum, on one silent city in the cliffs. Along the mesa top he showed them mounds under which, still unexcavated, lay the civilization of a people. Telling how, in the eleventh century, some fear drove this people from the mesa top down into the canyons, Nusbaum led the Rockefellers through crevices and up toe holds pecked in the sheer rock to Cliff Palace, Balcony House and other great ruins — towers, terraces, whole towns built into caves. Toward the end of the thirteenth century, tree rings show a drought that lasted twenty-four years. Leaving their houses empty in the cliffs, their temple to the Sun unfinished, this people wandered away, searching for water, to mingle with other tribes.

Aware of what Nusbaum's interpretation had meant to himself and his boys, Mr. Rockefeller asked how much Congress had appropriated for the museum. "Not a cent," said Nusbaum; a friend in San Francisco had given $5,000. "I want to contribute," said Mr. Rockefeller, "and help you demonstrate the merits of your museum project, with the understanding, of course, that it is properly a government responsibility, and that the government will carry the load after private means has established its merit. If you feel it would benefit your plans to make any public announcement of private funds received, just say they were given by an interested but anonymous friend of the Parks."

The museum, today one of the finest in the National Parks, is where understanding and exploring Mesa Verde begin.

*Visitors instructed at the museum may visit
the mesa-top ruins by themselves;
they may climb down to the cliff dwellings
only when guided by a ranger.
Here a ranger points out a route to follow.*

*A series of dioramas, accompanied by baskets, feather cloaks, jewels and mummies
found during excavations, make clear the successive cultures through which the cliff dwellers evolved.*

*Guiding young and old down into the ruins, rangers who
are trained archaeologists bring a vanished people back to life.*

Grand Canyon, perhaps the most
remarkable geologic phenomenon
in the world, was one of the
National Park areas that ultimately
benefited from the museum pilot project.
It was in the hope that museums
could be established later in
such places that Mr. Rockefeller
originally supported the pilot project
at Mesa Verde, to demonstrate its
practicability and usefulness.
The Grand Canyon Museum was
established with the aid of the
Laura Spelman Rockefeller Memorial.

Yavapai Point juts from the South Rim; the museum there has been described as "a window through which you look into the Canyon from an unusually favorable place."

AS THE GRAND CANYON of the Colorado is approached from either rim, the earth suddenly opens, to sink down, age by geologic age, precipice after glowing precipice, to the river running — as small from this height as a thread — through dark rocks two billion years old, formed in the earth's first cooling. Mountains rise in the same shapes that men the world over, throughout time, have built their temples. Storms rage below while a visitor stands on the rim in sunlight. The North Rim is a mountain forest where conifers and aspen enclose exquisite meadows; the South is largely desert. No one can look into the Grand Canyon without wondering about its mysteries.

With the Grand Canyon behind him, a ranger tells visitors how it was formed.

92

Lining up to look through binoculars fixed on points of interest, visitors discover for themselves the actual places mentioned by the ranger in his talk.

A relief map shows a section of the vast watershed drained by the Colorado.

From museum displays at Yavapai visitors learn of the effect of the canyon on animal life of the region.

At Old Faithful Museum,
some rocks are soft; some, like silica,
are so hard they withstand explosions
and force geysers up into the air.

Yellowstone's marvels, scattered among
mountains often eleven thousand feet high,
cover more than two million acres.
A relief map is a help.

YELLOWSTONE — so fabulous that Congress needed photographs before it could believe that explorers and scientists weren't exaggerating even more than the scouts and trappers who preceded them — was created in 1872 as the first National Park "for the benefit and enjoyment of the people." Its huge geysers, gemlike pools, crystalline terraces, and the steaming cone in the cold lake are part of its volcanic wonders. Others are cliffs of black glass, a mountain wherein twelve forests — each in turn covered by ash and lava and through the ages petrified — stand on top of each other, and the huge and brilliant canyon down which the river plunges in great falls. Museums and trailside exhibits now guide and inform millions of visitors.

Old Faithful, erupting almost hourly in a steaming fountain
a hundred and fifty feet high, has become the symbol of Yellowstone.

*Anglers for trout,
who line the Fishing Bridge
even at night, find the nearby
museum a help in understanding
the fish, birds, animals and
geology of Yellowstone Lake.*

*The exhibits help visitors to identify
the two hundred species of Yellowstone birds.*

*Gulls, sandpipers, pelicans and other
sea birds live in these mountain waters.*

AT FISHING BRIDGE MUSEUM, visitors learn about the animal life around them. Yellowstone is one of the largest wildlife refuges in the world. Many species, once so hunted they were feared extinct, are here reviving. Quiet watchers on the trails may see antelope flash past, or eagles and bighorn sheep among the peaks, or, on lonely pools, one of the last of the trumpeter swans lead forth a trail of cygnets.

96

AT NORRIS BASIN MUSEUM, thermal phenomena are explained: a mile underground seethe great masses of superheated magma that once produced volcanoes. Cold water, seeping down, meets vapors so hot it flashes into steam and roars upward, to explode in soft rock, causing caverns below and terraces above. At intervals ranging from minutes to decades, the water surges up through hard rock into huge columns.

From broad safe paths, visitors learn about the natural history
of geysers, hot springs and mud volcanoes, as they observe them.

The museum porch overlooks this most active of the geyser basins.

Diagrams illustrate the subterranean causes of geyser action.

In 1924 Mr. Rockefeller found the fallen trees, brush and stones heaped along Yellowstone roadsides by the road builders detracting from the scenery and preventing new growth.

TO THE YOUNG NATIONAL PARK SERVICE, roads were urgent and money was scarce. Repeatedly, Congress failed to grant funds for such matters as clearing roadsides. Always interested in roads, Mr. Rockefeller wrote Superintendent Albright that he would like to finance clearing a small section of road in order to prove the importance of such practice. Picking one mile of very bad road, another about average, and a third needing only a little help, Albright got to work and sent photographs made before and after. The improvement was so great that during the next five years Mr. Rockefeller gave $50,000 to clearing Yellowstone roadsides. By then Congress was convinced, and clearing Park roadsides became a national policy.

This photograph, made immediately after clearing, shows what a barrier, mental as well as physical, has been removed.

By 1926, when Mr. Rockefeller returned, wild flowers already lined the roads; today conifers and aspens have sprung up.

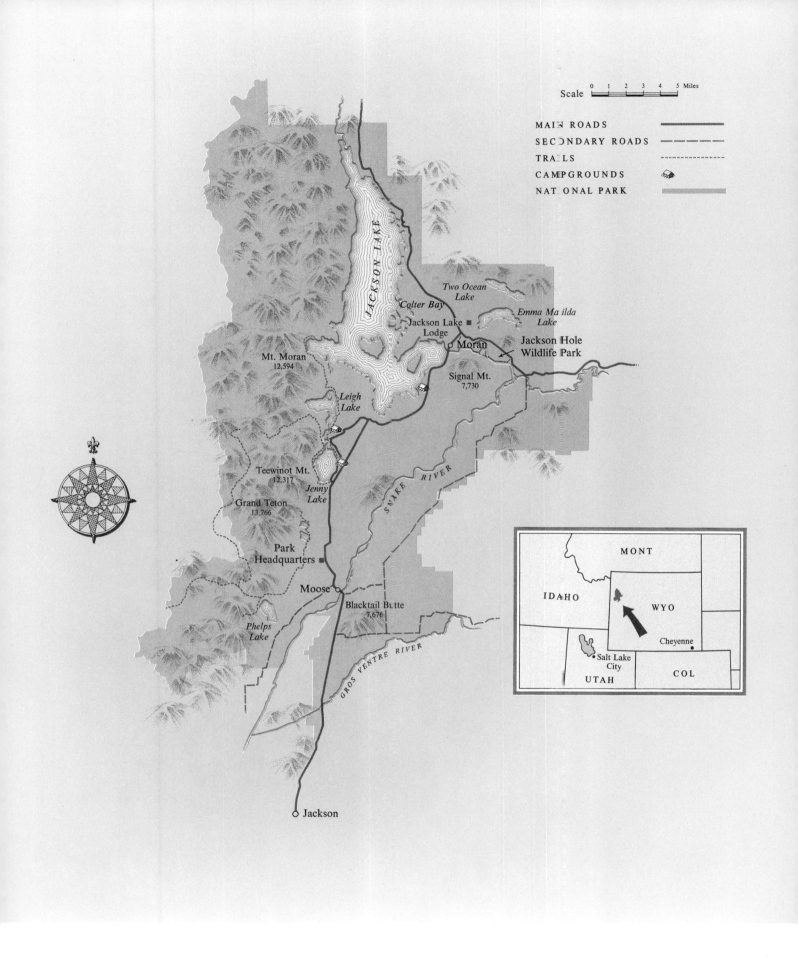

Scale 0 1 2 3 4 5 Miles

MAIN ROADS
SECONDARY ROADS
TRAILS
CAMPGROUNDS
NATIONAL PARK

JACKSON LAKE

Two Ocean Lake

Colter Bay

Emma Matilda Lake

Jackson Lake Lodge

Moran

Jackson Hole Wildlife Park

Mt. Moran
12,594

Signal Mt.
7,730

Leigh Lake

Teewinot Mt.
12,317

Jenny Lake

SNAKE RIVER

Grand Teton
13,766

Park Headquarters

Moose

Blacktail Butte
7,676

Phelps Lake

GROS VENTRE RIVER

Jackson

MONT

IDAHO

WYO

Cheyenne

Salt Lake City

UTAH

COL

THE GRAND TETONS

THE GRAND TETONS, a cluster of huge peaks forty miles long, are one of the most spectacular mountain ranges in America. Carved by glaciers from a great block fault caused by earthquakes, they tower up to the thirteen-thousand-foot Grand Teton, and dominate the horizon of Wyoming. In 1926 Superintendent Albright took Mr. and Mrs. Rockefeller and three of the boys on a two-day trip into the Teton country. From the low hills around Jackson Hole they saw the Tetons in their full majesty. "Returning in the afternoon to Yellowstone Park," wrote Albright, "I took . . . the old wagon trail along the bluff overlooking the Snake River. There is a high point along this bluff from which one can view the entire valley . . . The shadows of the Tetons were already reaching across the river bottoms . . . but the distant hills . . . were still bathed in sunshine from a clear sky." Here Mr. Albright told the Rockefellers of the long fight to make the Tetons a National Park and save from exploitation their natural setting — the lakes and valley of northern Jackson Hole.

Here and there this scenery — which the Rockefellers thought "equalled or surpassed anything they had ever beheld" — was marred by various structures built on private holdings. Mr. Rockefeller asked if he might have a map of these holdings, together with the probable cost of acquiring them to give back to the Government. Arriving that winter in New York with the maps and estimates, Mr. Albright was astonished to learn that Mr. Rockefeller had in mind saving the entire Jackson Hole Basin.

Few projects were more challenging to Mr. Rockefeller. Misunderstanding and controversy over the Park program developed. A Senate investigation was undertaken in 1932, and determined that the Park program was in the public interest and that complaints were without foundation. But, although the Grand Tetons became a National Park in 1929, it was not until 1950 that the Park was extended to include the greater portion of Jackson Hole Basin, over 30,000 acres of which were acquired and given the Government by Mr. Rockefeller; and the project was at last nearing completion.

Trail in the Grand Tetons.

John Colter, who in 1806 left the
returning Lewis and Clark Expedition
to trap beaver and explore the country,
was probably the first white man
to see the Tetons.

David Jackson, a mountain man who
wintered here in 1829, loved the place
so much his trapper partner
called it Jackson's Hole.

104

*Not until the 1880's
did homesteaders come
to Jackson Hole.
Long before the 1920's
they learned that
the country was too high,
cold and barren
for successful farming.*

*Cleared of abandoned sheds
and farm equipment,
the woods and meadows
returned to their best use:
range for wildlife,
recreation for people.*

EARLY IN THE 1920's, ranchers were urging that the Government buy back their holdings and make Jackson Hole a recreational area. Hope after hope of commercial exploitation flickered out. An irrigation dam spoiled Jackson Lake and piled its shores with dead wood; lumbering off the Tetons would jam the Snake River with timber easier and cheaper to get elsewhere; asbestos and other minerals existed in greater quantities in more accessible places — and all would ruin the principal asset Jackson Hole had: its beauty.

MANY HOLDINGS came up for sale during the Depression. Mr. Rockefeller directed that all landholders receive a fair price and that their personal circumstances be considered. Most were more than satisfied. Opposition came chiefly from cattlemen who saw more free grazing lands being withdrawn. The controversy was another incident in the long war involving three ideas: exploitation for gain, conservation for use, and conservation "for the benefit and enjoyment of the people."

The owner of this sawmill was one of those who urged that Jackson Hole be made a Park.

After removal of the old lumber, wild flowers returned to the fields, and trees to the cutover ridges.

Moose, largest and least wary of the deer family, are often seen feeding in the swamps and river bottoms around Jackson Hole.

One of the rivers of the Jackson Hole country is named after the buffalo that can still be seen in the Wildlife Park.

"THE TWO REASONS," Mr. Rockefeller explained, "which have moved me to consider this project are: 1st, The marvelous scenic beauty of the Teton Mountains and the Lakes at their feet, which are seen at their best from the Jackson Hole Valley; and 2nd, The fact that this Valley is the natural and necessary sanctuary and feeding place for the game which inhabits Yellowstone Park and the surrounding region. I am told that only through the preservation as a sanctuary of the Jackson Hole country can the buffalo, elk, moose and other animals be permanently maintained and preserved from extinction in the West."

Antelope, buffalo, moose, elk and mule deer — the big game for which Jackson Hole has been famous since the days of the mountain men — may now be seen browsing in the Wildlife Park, opened in 1948.

A newborn elk calf has no scent and instinctively lies so motionless it is seldom discovered. The elk herd at Jackson Hole is the largest big-game herd left in the United States.

Built among pine and aspens on a low bluff above the valley, Jackson Lake Lodge looks across the lake toward towering Mount Moran and other peaks of the Teton Range.

YEARLY, as Jackson Hole was restored more and more toward its original beauty, more and more people flocked to see it. By 1946 it had become, as ex-President Herbert Hoover observed, "one of the greatest recreational grounds in the whole of the United States." Hundreds of thousands came; in 1953 nearly a million came. Demand for accommodations far outran local facilities.

This need also Mr. Rockefeller prepared to meet. In 1940 he had formed Jackson Hole Preserve, Inc., "a non-profit, charitable and educational endeavor to aid in conserving areas of outstanding primitive grandeur and natural beauty, and to help make such areas available for enjoyment by the public."

Through Jackson Hole Preserve, funds were given to other conservation projects throughout the United States and its territories, including grants to help preserve the cypress trees of Florida, and St. John Island in the Caribbean. In Jackson Hole, the Preserve made possible the Wildlife Park with its laboratory, the restoration of historic buildings, the gift of matching funds to help purchase private holdings still within Park boundaries. In 1952 Mr. Rockefeller gave to Jackson Hole Preserve $6,000,000, which was used to build a hotel and cottages near Jackson Lake, and then helped the National Park Service develop low-cost accommodations near Colter Bay. In 1955, when Jackson Lake Lodge opened, 1,104,725 visitors came to the Grand Tetons. And nearly every summer Mr. Rockefeller himself returns, often to go up to his favorite spot on Lunch Tree Hill and look at "quite the grandest and most spectacular mountains I have ever seen . . . a picture of ever-changing beauty which is to me beyond compare."

*A temporary scaffolding was run up to the same height as the lounge floor of the
proposed Lodge so that Mr. Rockefeller and his associates could be certain that the Lodge
would afford visitors the best view possible of the Tetons.*

*The magnificent sweep of the Tetons is visible through the two-story picture windows
in the lounge and dining room of the Lodge.*

The Tetons rank with the Alps in the delight and the challenge they offer mountaineers. Here an expert, rappelling down in Cascade Canyon, bounds down the cliff.

The fighting trout of these mountain waters are a stimulating challenge to fishermen.

Alpine flora and abundant wildlife make the Tetons a paradise for naturalists.

Motorboats speed across Jenny Lake at all hours of the day, and often on moonlit nights.

Over a hundred miles of trails loop up through the Tetons and through the surrounding country. Here riders splash across the Snake, so swift and powerful it can be forded only in late summer and early fall.

113

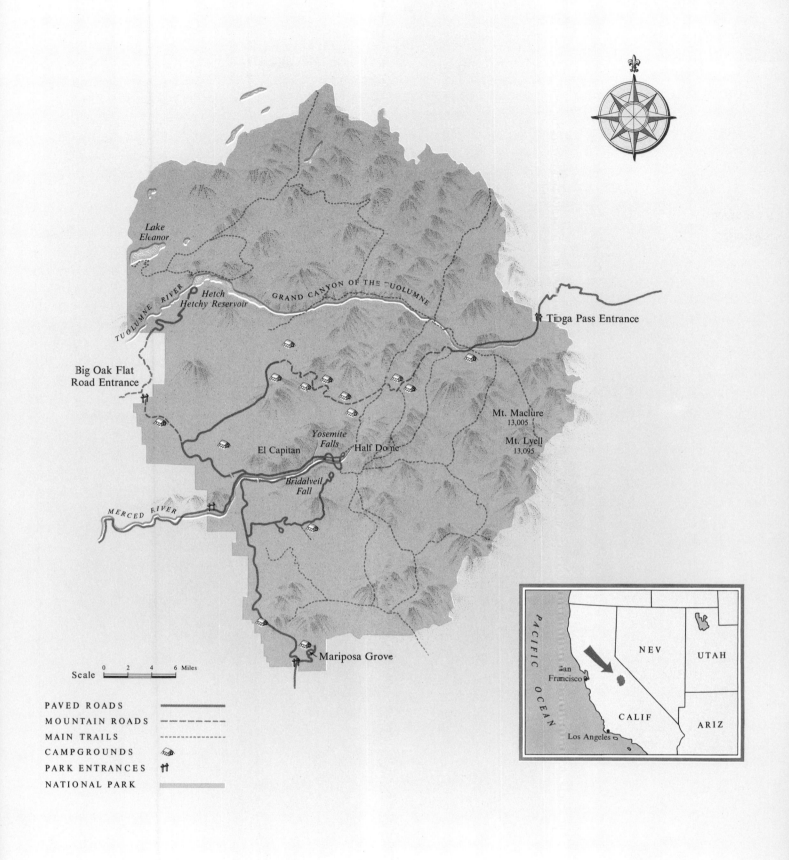

Lake
Eleanor

TUOLUMNE RIVER
Hetch
Hetchy Reservoir
GRAND CANYON OF THE TUOLUMNE
Tioga Pass Entrance

Big Oak Flat
Road Entrance

Mt. Maclure
13,005

Yosemite
Falls
El Capitan   Half Dome

Mt. Lyell
13,095

Bridalveil
Fall

MERCED RIVER

Mariposa Grove

Scale   0   2   4   6 Miles

PAVED ROADS
MOUNTAIN ROADS
MAIN TRAILS
CAMPGROUNDS
PARK ENTRANCES
NATIONAL PARK

PACIFIC OCEAN

San Francisco

NEV   UTAH

CALIF

Los Angeles   ARIZ

YOSEMITE

YOSEMITE was created as a park in 1864 by an Act of Congress, signed by President Lincoln, setting aside Yosemite Valley and the Mariposa Grove of Big Trees "to be held inviolate" by the State of California. The park then did not include the surrounding peaks of the High Sierra or the alpine meadows that lay along their slopes. When John Muir, a young naturalist, arrived in California in 1868, he saw sheep ravaging the meadows like "hoofed locusts" and the "tree-slaughter" of the sawmills leveling the forests. Yearly he saw the Valley and the high country grow barer. To save the wild beauty of the region, he began to write books and articles urging his countrymen to protect the majestic mountains surrounding the areas of the original state park. This Congress did by creating the National Park in 1890. California re-ceded Yosemite Valley and the Mariposa Grove in 1906. Thus, as a result of Muir's labors, Yosemite National Park embraced the Valley and Grove as well as the mountains. Lying on the west slope of the Sierra Nevada, Yosemite was best described by Muir: "It contains countless lakes and waterfalls and smooth, silky lawns. Here, too, are the noblest forests, the highest granite domes, the deepest ice-carved canyons, and snowy mountains soaring into the sky twelve and thirteen thousand feet. On these high slopes wild-flower gardens grow in the sun, and glaciers work silently in the shadows."

The approach to this incomparable country from the northwest was in danger of becoming a desolation of stumps. Then Nicholas Roosevelt, the conservationist, wrote an editorial in 1928 describing the denuding of fine stands of sugar pine. From his experiences in other regions similarly threatened, Mr. Rockefeller recognized a situation calling for prompt action. Offering to match any funds provided by the Government to add the forests to Yosemite National Park control, Mr Rockefeller gave $1,750,000 toward the purchase of over 15,000 acres of heavily timbered lands. By 1930, after sixty-six years of effort by Congress, by such ardent conservationists as Muir and Nicholas Roosevelt, by the efforts and contributions of citizens and local government, the full integration of Yosemite was practically accomplished.

Merced River in Yosemite.

THE FORESTS OF YOSEMITE change as the Sierra rises. From steep, hot canyons where Digger pines give no shade in summer, one enters cool groves of bay trees, oaks and pines at the Park boundary; from there to timber line, where mountain junipers cling to glacier-polished slopes, one marvelous forest succeeds another. Coming in by Big Oak Flat, the visitor passes the rarest and most magnificent trees of all: towering sugar pines, upwards of two hundred feet high, and the more massive Sierra Redwoods — both trees survivors of an earlier age and once threatened with extinction. The importance of Big Oak Flat "as a scientific laboratory for the study of natural forest conditions, as a region of great educational and recreational value, and as a breathing space for the nation," according to the Department of the Interior, "cannot be measured in dollars and cents, for in a relatively few years there will be no other forest like it."

Storm-twisted, the ancient Jeffrey pine on Sentinel Dome looks over Yosemite Valley to the peaks and domes of the High Sierra.

Sugar pines, their highest branches weighted by immense cones, grow best at altitudes of three to seven thousand feet.

The beauty of Yosemite, like that of all great places, lies in the sum total of all one sees, feels, touches, understands. It lies also in contrasts: Bridalveil Fall plunging 620 feet into mist, the sheer granite of El Capitan, the green forests and meadows beside the clear Merced River.

THE PARKS THEMSELVES are vast museums outdoors. They are alive and therefore ever-changing. Storm and sun, life and death, uplift and erosion are still at work in them. But to see fully the dynamics of a region as they can seldom or never be seen outdoors requires a museum within walls. Here in an hour or two, one can see how geologic forces worked, how ecologies change, and bird, beast and plant change with them, what people lived here, and how and why. In the parks, an indoor museum is an introduction to what one meets outside.

In the Yosemite Museum, originally aided by the Laura Spelman Rockefeller Memorial, the visitor can learn to identify the brilliant shades of butterflies, or the intricate shapes of leaves, or the look of different minerals in the rock; learn to recognize that the bird diving near a waterfall is a water ousel, or that the strange scarlet tip near a melting snowdrift is a snow plant, or that the huge pine, by its gesture and its giant cones, is a sugar pine.

Here, too, is information on more than seven hundred miles of trails, around the Valley and up in the high country: whether there is still snow at Tenaya Lake; whether the wild irises are out yet at Tuolumne Meadows; whether a group is being organized to make a long expedition up the trails.

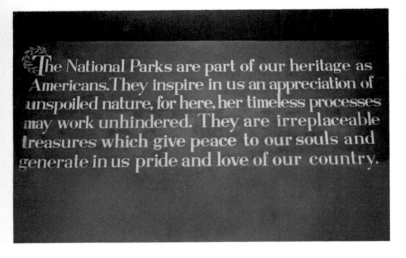

*Over a museum doorway, the purpose of
the Parks is stated in letters of gold.*

*Muir's battered tin cup rests where he, like all
mountaineers, must often have placed it —
in the crotch of a timber-line tree.*

Behind the museum rises
the huge mountain wall
from which Yosemite Falls plunges
1,430 feet in its first leap.

The library houses not only
books but paintings, photographs
and memorabilia of the many
artists, scientists and historians
Yosemite and the Sierra have inspired.

Relief maps show how Yosemite Valley was formed and where
it lies among the peaks and other canyons of the Sierra Nevada.

123

Campfire talks, held out under the trees and the stars, are illustrated with slides and movies.

TO HELP PEOPLE from all over America and the world understand and enjoy what they are seeing, the Park Service offers many tours and classes in the open. But the great delight is to form a group and go up into the high country, to climb its peaks, to camp out among alpine flowers beside glacial lakes and waterfalls, and to explore magnificent canyons unreached by any road.

A live and harmless little snake in the hands of the ranger naturalist delights an afternoon session of the Junior Nature School.

From near Glacier Point, a ranger explains how the Sierra was formed:
how rivers cut steeper canyons between the rising mountains, and glaciers,
thousands of feet deep, shaped the Valley into a U and sheared away the face of Half Dome.

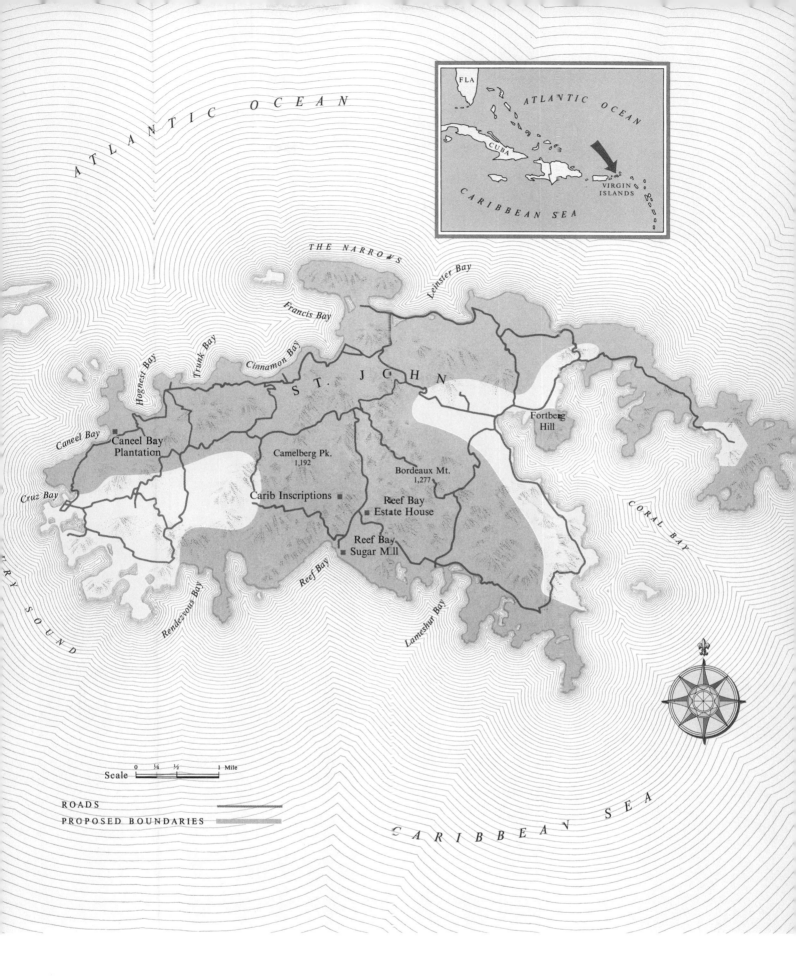

ATLANTIC OCEAN

THE NARROWS

Francis Bay

Leinster Bay

Hogner Bay

Trunk Bay

Cinnamon Bay

S T .   J O H N

Caneel Bay

Fortberg
Hill

Caneel Bay
Plantation

Camelberg Pk.
1,192

Bordeaux Mt.
1,277

Cruz Bay

Carib Inscriptions

Reef Bay
Estate House

CORAL BAY

Reef Bay
Sugar Mill

Rendezvous Bay

Reef Bay

Lameshur Bay

RY SOUND

Scale   0   ¼   ½   1 Mile

ROADS
PROPOSED BOUNDARIES

CARIBBEAN SEA

ATLANTIC OCEAN

FLA

CUBA

VIRGIN
ISLANDS

CARIBBEAN SEA

VIRGIN ISLANDS

THE VIRGIN ISLANDS NATIONAL PARK will occupy two-thirds of St. John, smallest and least populous of the three principal islands that make up the American Virgin Islands. The white sands of St. John's beaches contrast dramatically with the deep blue of the Caribbean and the tropical green of the flora that covers 85 per cent of the island's 19.2 square miles. One of the Lesser Antilles group of the West Indies, St. John is a volcanic creation characterized by steep mountains, pleasant valleys, many bays and a gentle climate averaging 78 degrees. Its spectacular sunsets are noted for a magnificent afterglow that colors the eastern sky as well.

The island was first seen by a European when Columbus sighted the Virgin Islands and named them after the eleven thousand virgins of Saint Ursula. At that time St. John was inhabited by Carib Indians, who probably migrated from South America and who left behind petroglyphs — stone writings that still fascinate archaeologists. Possibly driven from the island by the Spaniards in the sixteenth century, the Caribs were gone when the first European settlers came in 1684. A permanent colony of Danes came in 1717, established sugar plantations, and built a prosperous society. The Danish plantation civilization came to an end in the 1800's when slavery was abolished, and the island passed to American ownership in 1917.

St. John was first studied as a possible National Park by the Department of the Interior in the late 1930's. Following World War II, Laurance S. Rockefeller acquired Caneel Bay Estate, a small resort area on the west coast of St. John. In 1954, impressed by the promising possibilities of the island as a Park — reported in a 1939 survey for the Park Service — he led an effort to acquire five thousand acres of St. John to offer the United States for a National Park. The project was envisioned both as a means of saving the island from future haphazard exploitation and to help advance the economy of the Virgin Islands. John D. Rockefeller, Jr., joined his son in making funds available to Jackson Hole Preserve, Inc., to buy the land. The property was accepted by Congress in 1956 to form the Virgin Islands National Park.

Sunset off St. John Island.

At Peter Durlieu's plantation house on Caneel Bay, Danish settlers crowded in refuge during a violent revolt by their slaves in 1733. The revolt was finally suppressed by French soldiers from Martinique.

HISTORIC RUINS recall St. John's eighteenth-century Danish colony, centered around Reef Bay on the south of the island, Coral Bay on the east, and Caneel Bay on the west. First colonizers in 1717 numbered twenty planters and five soldiers, but within a few years three thousand settlers were living a comfortable and profitable life on sugar plantations. The idyllic life of the planters lasted until slavery was abolished in the 1800's. Without slave labor, the plantation economy collapsed, and the planters left the island, never to return. Today the haunted ruins evoke once more a brief and remote civilization that has not yet been fully researched and reported by historians.

The sugar mills were built by the Danes to process the colony's one product for export.

A fort, commanding Coral Bay from a peninsula summit, was built by the Danes to keep out British ships.

131

From the veranda of the Reef Bay Estate House, the planter could look out across his land toward the Caribbean.

Christianity was brought to St. John by Moravian missionaries in the 1700's. Churches were built at Coral and Cruz Bays.

Some of the early Danish settlers lie buried on St. John. The surviving settlers left the island when the plantation economy fell.

The heights of St. John provide a remarkable panorama of sky, sea and islands, once the refuge of pirates, who found the excellent harbors ideal anchorages. Danish war vessels also used the coves for mooring during Danish ownership of the islands. In 1917, St. John Island, together

with St. Thomas and St. Croix, was bought from Denmark by the United States. Of the three,
the larger islands of St. Thomas and St. Croix have been developed economically,
but St. John remains virtually unchanged since the Danish planters left over a century ago.

AN ISLAND OF PRIMITIVE BEAUTY, St. John was surveyed by the Park Service as a possible National Park almost twenty years ago, when a careful appraisal was made of its natural and historical features and its recreational possibilities. Since that time the island has remained uncrowded and unspoiled. Transportation and living accommodations for visitors have been provided without marring the island. There are guest facilities at Caneel, Trunk and Cruz Bays.

Lameshur Bay on the southern coast of St. John looks out over the Caribbean to St. Croix.

St. John has many trails but few roads.
This one has been improved to
permit passage by jeep.

*Further plans for Caneel Bay Plantation are explained to a
representative group of islanders by Laurance S. Rockefeller (extreme left).*

137

THE SHELTERED BEACHES of St. John rim unusually clear water. Ideal for swimming, skin-diving, sailing and fishing, the island induces visitors to stay, not for just hours, but for days and weeks. Caneel Bay Plantation, sponsored by Jackson Hole Preserve, provides some accommodations for visitors.

Caneel Bay is on the northern end of the western coast of St. John, thirty minutes by boat from St. Thomas.

Sailboats venture into Sir Francis Drake Channel, toward the British Virgin Islands.

The beach at Trunk Bay is inviting to conchologists, who are attracted by the variety and color of sea shells found on the shores of St. John Island.

PART THREE:

TRIUMPHS OF NATURE AND OF MAN

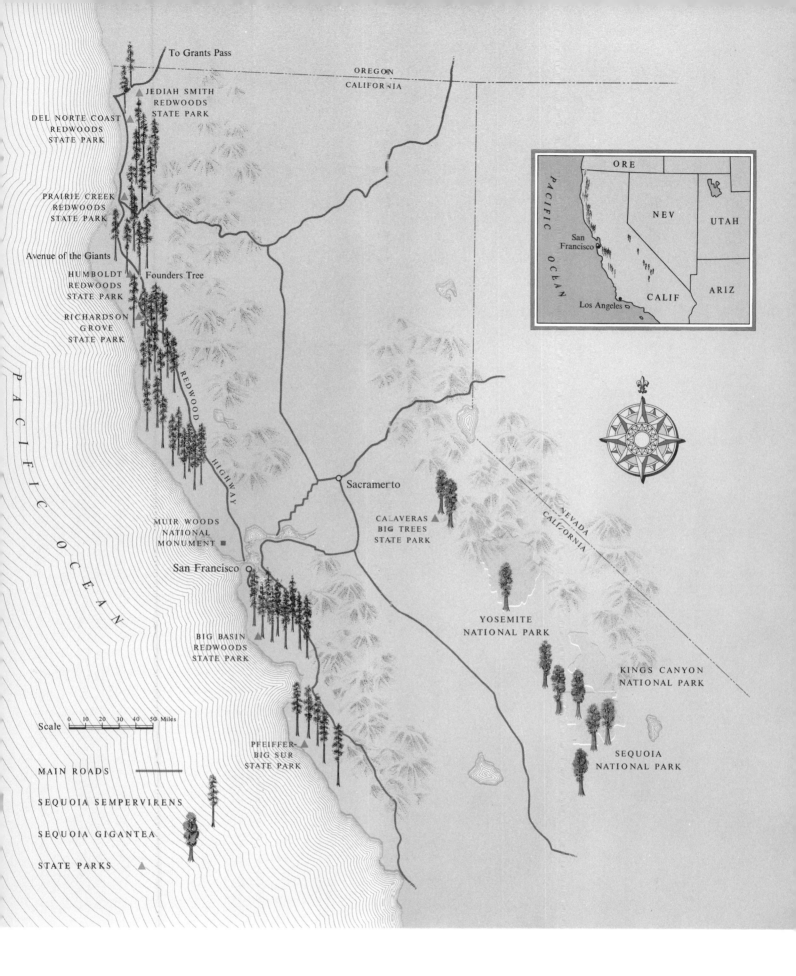

To Grants Pass

OREGON
CALIFORNIA

JEDIAH SMITH
REDWOODS
STATE PARK

DEL NORTE COAST
REDWOODS
STATE PARK

PRAIRIE CREEK
REDWOODS
STATE PARK

Avenue of the Giants

HUMBOLDT
REDWOODS   Founders Tree
STATE PARK

RICHARDSON
GROVE
STATE PARK

REDWOOD

HIGHWAY

Sacramento

MUIR WOODS
NATIONAL
MONUMENT

CALAVERAS
BIG TREES
STATE PARK

San Francisco

BIG BASIN
REDWOODS
STATE PARK

YOSEMITE
NATIONAL PARK

KINGS CANYON
NATIONAL PARK

0 10 20 30 40 50 Miles
Scale

MAIN ROADS

PFEIFFER-
BIG SUR
STATE PARK

SEQUOIA
NATIONAL PARK

SEQUOIA SEMPERVIRENS

SEQUOIA GIGANTEA

STATE PARKS

PACIFIC OCEAN

PACIFIC OCEAN

ORE

NEV   UTAH

San
Francisco

CALIF   ARIZ

Los Angeles

NEVADA
CALIFORNIA

THE REDWOODS

REDWOODS OF CALIFORNIA are the oldest, tallest, largest living things on the face of the earth. Native today to parts of the Pacific coast, the Redwoods are prehistoric survivals, their direct ancestry going back millions of years. Resistant alike to disease and to fire, they attain fabulous ages, ranging from 1,000 to 3,000 years. Named "Redwoods" by Spanish explorers in 1769, they were given the scientific name of "Sequoia" in 1847 in honor of the Cherokee Indian. The coastal Redwoods are identified as *Sequoia sempervirens* (ever-living trees), and the Sierra Redwoods as *Sequoia gigantea* (big trees). The coastal species are generally the taller, growing to heights of 364 feet — about the height of a thirty-five-story skyscraper. The Sierra Redwoods attain a much wider girth, sometimes over thirty feet.

Of the Redwoods, John Muir wrote, "Through all the eventful centuries . . . God has cared for these trees, saved them from drought, disease, avalanches, and a thousand storms; but He cannot save them from sawmills and fools; this is left to the American people." Muir wrote in 1899, when trees that were a thirty-century triumph of nature were destroyed by man in a matter of days. To lumbermen the Redwoods were miracles of production: one tree contained 600,120 board feet of lumber — enough to build forty five-room houses.

The campaign to save the "Big Trees" got under way with the establishment of Sequoia, General Grant and Yosemite National Parks in 1890 — all preserving stands of the Sierra Redwoods. But, except for four small groves, the coastal Redwoods were still unprotected in 1918. That year the Save-the-Redwoods League was started, and eventually raised $6,000,000, of which a third was contributed by the state and another third by Mr. Rockefeller, Jr., who visited the forest and came away "speechless with admiration" at "anything so beautiful as the forests we came through today." Years later, in 1954, 5,760 acres of the oldest and largest trees across the continent from California — the Bald Cypresses of Florida — were saved by the National Audubon Society, aided by Jackson Hole Preserve and other contributors.

Rockefeller Redwood Forest at Bull Creek Flat.

ON THE MORNING of March 13, 1933, a 320-foot, 500-ton tree (*at left*), over twelve centuries old, crashed to the ground in Richardson Grove on the California coast. A combination of fire, wind and rain-softened ground had finally brought natural death to the ancient tree.

From the markings on the stump section (*lower right*), botanists determined the natural history of the fallen tree. The great natural enemy of the tree was fire, which first attacked it severely in 1147, when the tree was 447 years old — still the period of youth in the life of a Redwood. Other fires left their scars: in 1595, 1789, 1806, 1820 and four times thereafter. The unconquerable tree, scarred, cracked by weakness from the first fire, dead on one side, continued to grow.

Rings on the tree (*lower left*) show its size at specific ages down through the centuries. The tree was born in the early 700's A.D., when Justinian II ruled the Roman Empire. By the Norman Conquest in 1066, it had attained a third of its girth. When Columbus discovered America, it had passed the half-way mark in its growth. The tree was in its maturity during our colonial period and slipped into old age at the time of the Civil War. Its life spanned the history of man from the eve of the Holy Roman Empire of Charlemagne to the European rumblings that led to World War II.

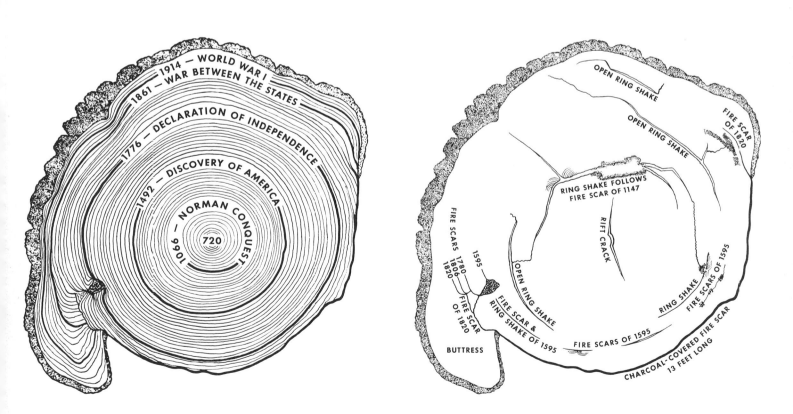

DIAMETER OF TREE — 12 FEET

For the skeptical, who had heard of but not seen the Redwoods, cross sections were shipped across the country to help convince Americans of the natural wonders of the Redwood forests.

THE REDWOODS were first discovered by modern Americans in the 1850's and rapidly became famous. Always intrigued by the natural wonders of the Pacific coast, visitors made excursions to see the trees and looked for ways to dramatize their immense size in photographs for the benefit of those back home. Mark Twain, U. S. Grant, Henry Ward Beecher, Horatio Alger, and hundreds of other notables visited the trees.

It took five men 22 days to fell a Redwood in the 1850's. The sizes of the trees were dramatized by groups who danced, sat, or stood on them.

*Early visitors went to all kinds
of extremes to return home
with pictorial evidence
of the Redwoods' giant size.*

*In 1881 a tunnel was cut to permit a road to go through a Redwood called the Wawona Tree.
The tree is still alive, but such trick treatments are now forbidden.*

149

ALTHOUGH THE NATIONAL PARKS in the Sierras were authorized in 1890, money to buy the Redwoods from private owners had to be raised. Members of the National Geographic Society, garden clubs, private subscriptions saved the *Sequoia gigantea*. After the Save-the-Redwoods League was organized to save the *Sequoia sempervirens*, the State of California, prominent leaders in American life, school children, clubs and societies raised enough money to buy 69,000 acres of the coastal Redwood forests. In 1954 the South Calaveras Grove of giant Redwoods was saved by the League in a special campaign aided by a $1,000,000 gift from Mr. Rockefeller.

Whole sections of the primitive Redwood forests were denuded by lumber operations. This area is part of the Prairie Creek State Park.

Saving the Redwoods was the result of the combined efforts of many dedicated men like Elmer Reynolds, Stephen Mather and Horace Albright (all mounted), who were active in the project as early as 1914.

Lumber was cut fast to meet the demands of California's rapidly growing population.

In 1931 the Save-the-Redwoods League and the Calaveras Grove Association
established Big Trees State Park, to which the South Calaveras Grove was added in 1954.
The groves are still among the most popular points of interest to West Coast visitors.

THE BALD CYPRESS TREES in Florida are the nation's oldest trees, next to the Redwoods. Of a cypress forest that millions of years ago covered 1,536,000 acres of Florida, a remnant patch of 5,760 acres called Corkscrew Swamp Sanctuary was saved by the National Audubon Society, aided by Jackson Hole Preserve and other contributors. Corkscrew Swamp is also a rookery, in which there are an estimated ten thousand nests: egrets, ibises, herons, snipes, cranes are among the hundred known birds in the sanctuary.

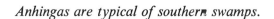

Anhingas are typical of southern swamps.

The egret was saved from extinction.

Corkscrew Swamp has a floating carpet of lettuce that grows only in water.

COLONIAL WILLIAMSBURG

COLONIAL WILLIAMSBURG was the capital of the Virginia colony during the valiant days when the quest for freedom united America in a war for independence, and the pattern of the new nation was forming in the intrepid minds of men like Jefferson, Madison and George Mason. Here flowered a brilliant civilization, evident in the dignity and beauty of its buildings, in the pride of its craftsmanship, in its spacious streets and gardens.

By the 1900's, although time had left the once lovely city scarred with the intrusions of later, more hurried eras, the spirit of its great past was not wholly gone from the quiet streets. The late Dr. W. A. R. Goodwin, Rector of Bruton Parish, as he went about his ministry in Williamsburg, was deeply aware of the immense meaning of the city to the American experience — the ringing defiance of Patrick Henry's words in the Capitol, the resolution leading to the Declaration of Independence, the creation of the model Bill of Rights, the drafting of the Statute for Religious Freedom. He began to dream of how a restored Williamsburg could evoke once more the bravery and faith of those golden days and speak across the years to new generations of Americans. "I am convinced," he said, "that from an historical point of view this is the greatest teaching opportunity which exists in America." After a series of discussions with Dr. Goodwin, beginning at a meeting of the Phi Beta Kappa Society in 1926, Mr. Rockefeller came to share his vision of an inspiring place where "the future may learn from the past," and enthusiastically carried out the work of restoring Williamsburg.

Thirty years later, more than 70 colonial buildings had been restored; about 400 more had been reconstructed; and some 700 post-colonial structures had been torn down or removed. The dream of Dr. Goodwin and the objective of Mr. Rockefeller had been advanced, in the words of the Trustees, "to re-create accurately the environment of the men and women of 18th-century Williamsburg and to bring about such an understanding of their lives and times that present and future generations may more vividly appreciate the contribution of these early Americans to the ideals and culture of our country."

The Duke of Gloucester Street.

Mr. Rockefeller and his associate,
Kenneth Chorley, President
of Colonial Williamsburg, Inc.,
(below a portrait of the original architects
of the $60,000,000 project) have worked
together for nearly thirty-five years.

During the early days of the restoration, property was
acquired in the name of Dr. Goodwin to preserve
the anonymity of Williamsburg's benefactor.

THE SUCCESS of the restoration of Williamsburg was rooted in the devotion
of conceiver and benefactor, historians, architects, engineers and administrators to
a common ideal expressed by one of the architects: "Reverently to preserve every
vestige of the old where it survives, preferably on its original site; where it does not,
to exhaust first every vestige of what the old was actually like; where this evidence
does not suffice, to work scrupulously in the style of the very time and place, yet
with artistic sensitiveness."

The dimensions of the restoration job are suggested by a small segment of the Duke of Gloucester Street as it was in the 1920's.

After the restoration, the same segment of the street looks once more as it did in Williamsburg's colonial days.

THE FIRST STEP of the restoration work was an immense and complicated job in research and detection to discover the architectural details of the old city. In Williamsburg, old foundations of buildings long gone were excavated, scores of tons of artifacts were sifted by archaeologists, old deeds were searched, wills, inventories and court records were studied painstakingly. The research extended from Williamsburg to England and — to find an original chandelier of the period — to China. Chemical tests were made of the original building materials so that the eighteenth-century formulas could be reconstructed and followed in the restoration work. Other studies in building methods eventually determined how shingles and bricks were laid and how joints were mortised. The quest for authenticity demanded three times the work in design and construction that new buildings require.

In the William and Mary College Library is an excellent guide to locations of vanished buildings,
a remarkably accurate billeting map of Williamsburg in 1782 — the work of a French Army engineer.

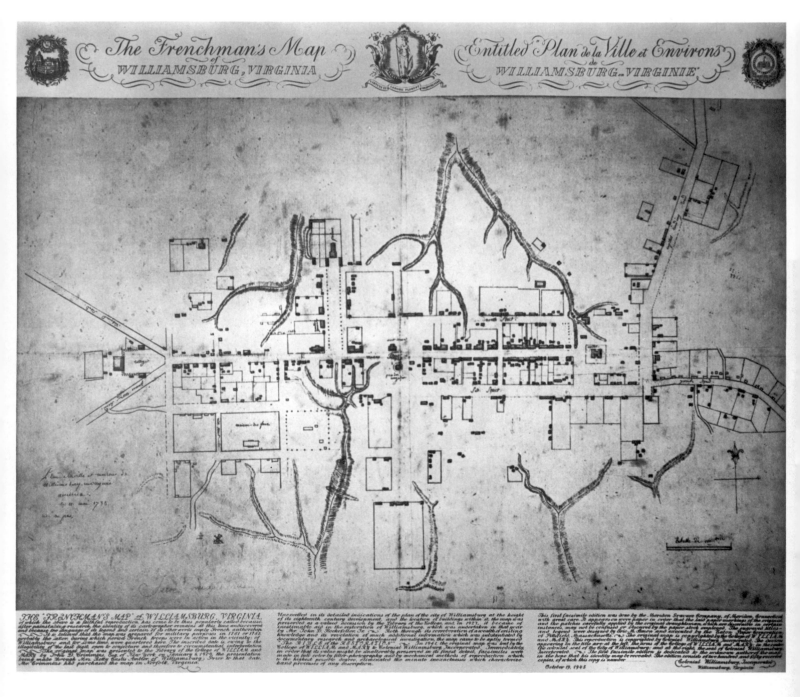

A copper plate found at the Bodleian Library, Oxford, England, depicted old college and public buildings.

Archaeologists combed excavations for evidences of the old city's life.

The Governor's Palace had burned, but the original foundation of the building was uncovered and aided immeasurably in the reconstruction of the great house.

161

*Dr. Goodwin and Mr. Rockefeller
followed the work on the site.
Mr. Rockefeller authorized the adherence
to the utmost authenticity, whatever the
cost in time, money or effort.*

BEFORE ACTUAL RESTORATION COULD BEGIN, lands comprising the area of the colonial city had to be acquired. Then buildings had to be carefully appraised, so that the largest number possible could be preserved by scrupulous restoration. Reconstruction was undertaken only when necessary to restore the old form. Meanwhile, during the prolonged procedures of property acquisitions, information on the architecture and furnishings of the colonial city was assembled at Williamsburg, workmen were trained in eighteenth-century methods, original lot and street lines were plotted.

*Non-colonial buildings
of no inherent or
historical value were razed.*

Some buildings were moved to locations outside the restored area.

Bricks were made of local clay in the same size, color and texture as the originals.

Restoration brickyards, using original methods, made many different sizes of brick.

The powder magazine, sixty years old at the beginning of the Revolution,
was emptied of its powder, by order of Royal Governor Lord Dunmore,
on the day following the Battle of Lexington, to prevent the colonists from seizing it.
In later years it was used variously as a market, dancing school, chapel and stable, but was
eventually saved by the Association for the Preservation of Virginia Antiquities.

The Red Lion, built in three stages in the eighteenth century as suggested by the three doors,
was opened in 1718 as an ordinary "with cleanly lodging and diet for travelers."
Old photographs, like the one at left, were of great help to architects in the restoration;
even more helpful was a 1743 sketch of the Red Lion surviving in court records,
where it had been introduced as evidence in a lawsuit.

In 1930 a scale model of the Capitol was built to indicate its original appearance.

THE ORIGINAL CAPITOL of the Virginia Colony was built in 1705. It burned in 1747. Its foundations had been preserved by the Association for the Preservation of Virginia Antiquities, which presented the site to Colonial Williamsburg. To the Virginia Assembly—meeting when the reconstructed Capitol was dedicated—Mr. Rockefeller said, "What a temptation to sit in silence and let the past speak to us of those great patriots whose voices once resounded in these halls and whose far-seeing wisdom, high courage and unselfish devotion to the common good will ever be an inspiration to noble living."

In 1934 the reconstructed Capitol was finished and opened to the public.

In 1932 the exterior of the Capitol was nearly completed.

Over the Governor's chair in the chamber of the General Court hangs Queen Anne's coat of arms.

History comes to life in a re-enactment in the House of Burgesses, most famous room in the Capitol.

Most of the houses of the colonial capital were small but
beautifully proportioned. Massive outside chimneys were characteristic.

Restoration of gardens was aided by
lists of plants in old letters and diaries.

Like most Williamsburg gardens, that of Wythe House, home of a signer
of the Declaration of Independence, tends to formality and architectural integration with the house.

167

In reconstructing the magnificent Governor's Palace, architects used three hundred pages of research, including a detailed floor plan drawn by Thomas Jefferson when Governor.

Voluminous inventories of two successive Governors were invaluable guides to such furnishings as those in the northeast bedroom.

*Original needlework seats, acquired
in London for the Restoration,
are on the Queen Anne chairs
in the "little dining room"
used by the Governor's family.*

*The Council of Virginia proposed in 1710 that
the upper middle room "be furnished with gilt leather hangings."*

COLONIAL WILLIAMSBURG is a living adventure in education, a city where not only the buildings and furnishings but the ways and customs of the past have been restored. Today in thirteen reconstructed shops, craftsmen skilled in eighteenth-century methods and the use of eighteenth-century tools make exact reproductions of colonial artifacts. "This is *good* history because it is *live* history," wrote a New York high school teacher.

The forge in the blacksmith's shop is fired by a great hand bellows, and the hot iron is hammered into shape on an old anvil.

In early days the blacksmith built coaches and giant wagon wheels as well as scores of household utensils.

170

The Pasteur-Galt Apothecary has colonial medicines, in delft jars, and antiquated surgical tools.

An eighteenth-century press turns out proclamations and handbills for Colonial Williamsburg.

At the Boot and Shoemaker's Shop hand-sewn shoes are made on wooden lasts.

*Over eight million Americans
have visited Colonial Williamsburg.*

THE MEANING OF WILLIAMSBURG has been best stated by its visitors. An Army private wrote, "Of all the sights I have seen, and the books I have read, and the speeches I have heard, none ever made me see the greatness of this country with more force and clearness than when I saw Williamsburg slumbering peacefully on its old foundations." President Eisenhower said, "I think no American could stand in these halls and on this spot without feeling a very great and deep sense of the debt we owe to the courage, the stamina, and the faith of our forefathers."

Servicemen have found Williamsburg deeply moving.

*Young people from 2,200 schools have come
to Williamsburg in two years.*

THE PURPOSE OF WILLIAMSBURG is to recall to the present and the future the dedicated men of the past whose eloquence and courage advanced human liberty. To remind us that liberty still has its champions, the Williamsburg Award was created in 1955 and was first awarded to Sir Winston Churchill.

EPILOGUE

IN 1924, when I first met Mr. Rockefeller, the National Park Service was scarcely eight years old. Men like Stephen T. Mather, first Director of the Service, Jesse L. Nusbaum, the Chief Archaeologist, and Arno B. Cammerer, Assistant Director, were still attempting, without adequate funds and with little precedent to guide them, to create a Park Service that would really serve the people in their enjoyment of the natural wonders of our land. I was superintendent of Yellowstone and also Assistant Director (Field) of the Service, and I know something from direct experience of the improvising and the stubborn persistence that were necessary to get things done in those days. I do not believe that they could have been done at all if a great many Americans had not shared that basic human compulsion to save what we prize for our fellows and for our children. This mission takes many forms of expression in different individuals. We have had eloquent spokesmen, who have talked and written with great effectiveness of some of the challenges of conservation. We have had men of organizational genius, who have rallied the people of the country in great voluntary associations to answer specific needs. We have had conscientious, perceptive men, who have quietly stepped in at critical times and turned the tide when everything seemed to be going against us.

Mr. Rockefeller is such a friend of our heritage. He brings to the problems of conservation a natural love of the beauties of nature, an alert, inquiring mind, a realistic and practical sense of pace and appropriateness. Moreover, as we have seen in this chronicle, he becomes active in these matters, not just giving financial support — critically important as it has been at times — but giving also long hours of thought and planning, ranging from the passionate interest in trees and drives that he showed as a boy at Forest Hill, to the vision and scope of his plans of a restored Williamsburg.

With some of these projects Mr. Rockefeller has been deeply and personally concerned for twenty, thirty and even forty years. Sometimes the project comes from his own perception of a need; sometimes from his instant recognition of the merit of a plan of others. He holds no brief for an idea because it is his; he has it checked as exhaustively as any other, and, when outvoted on a board, he can cheerfully and diligently participate in carrying out the modified decision. In any project, large or small, no matter how many claim his attention, he always insists on arriving at a clear and objective evaluation of what is involved. He follows through with infinite patience and a calm acceptance of the delays and frustrations that frequently attend projects that are new or large. No detail is too petty, no combination of factors too intricate, no scope too vast for his consideration. I have seen him put hours into the planning of roads and drives, going over the area with the thoroughness of an engineer and coming to grips with the multitude of practical factors that always intervene between the idea and the reality. In 1938 the American Society of Landscape Architects made him an honorary member — an exceptional action for a professional association, and a significant one.

There is, moreover, a philosophy in the way Mr. Rockefeller does things as well as in what he does. In the more than thirty years that I have been associated with him in many of the activities narrated in this book, he has always preferred to supplement, by his support and interest, efforts joined in by other Americans, acting in groups or individually or through their representatives in government. He believes, as his father did, that when a project is the ardent concern of many people with some stake in it, however small, it flourishes and fulfills its purpose.

Indeed, that is to me the real message and meaning of this book. There is as much to be said for Mr. Rockefeller's example as for his achievements. I have watched his sons, whom I met thirty years ago in Yellowstone, grow up to carry on the same watchful and active concern. Through the years, one by one they have taken up and carried on the continuing task of making the great values to be derived from our natural and historical heritage known and enjoyed by more and more people. Thus, they take their place beside their father and other conservationists who have been architects of natural preserves of national and international importance.

I hope that this book will lead more and more people to share in the responsibility of all of us as individuals to preserve our heritage. Many, through voluntary association, can give material support to conservation projects together that they could not give separately. Legislators intelligently concerned with conservation deserve and need wider support from more citizens who will take the trouble to inform themselves of new needs and weak spots in our conservation program.

Twenty years in the National Park Service, four of them as its Director, taught me the value of such citizens, no matter how little or how great their means. "Freedom," as Mr. Rockefeller once said, "does not come as a gift." Neither, as this book shows, do the great places that evoke in us some of the greatest experiences we know. They are among our most priceless possessions. They are ours, the heritage of every one of us. But they are also our responsibility. As *The New York Times* recently said editorially, "As our urban, mechanized society spreads itself with increasing speed and destructiveness across the land, the human need for preserving contact with natural areas, with living, wild and growing things, becomes more explicit and more pervasive. As natural areas rapidly diminish, the battle to keep the best of the remaining ones intact grows more intense."

I think this book will have achieved its mission if it leads others to just one conclusion, with regard to their common heritage, that Mr. Rockefeller reached long ago:

> "I believe that every right implies a responsibility·
> every opportunity an obligation; every possession a duty."

HORACE MARDEN ALBRIGHT

PICTURE CREDITS

When several pictures are on the same page, credits refer to top to bottom and left to right.

End Papers — Ansel Adams

Frontispiece — Ansel Adams

Contents — Thomas L. Williams, from
  Colonial Williamsburg

viii Karsh, Ottawa

4 E. W. Thorpe, courtesy of the
  City of Cleveland Heights

6 Perry Cragg, *Cleveland News*

7 From collection of
  Cleveland Plain Dealer

8 Courtesy of the
  City of Cleveland Heights

9 Courtesy of the City of East Cleveland

10 Courtesy of the
  City of Cleveland Heights

10 L. J. Sonkoy

11 L. J. Sonkoy

11 Perry Cragg, *Cleveland News*

12-13 Courtesy of the City of Cleveland

16 Gene Ahrens, from Shostal

18 Fairchild Aerial Surveys, Inc.

20 Brown Brothers

21 By permission of the estate of
  Alfred Stieglitz — Collection
  Museum of Modern Art

22 Brown Brothers

23-24 Palisades Interstate Park Commission

25 Weitner Aerophoto Service, Yonkers,
  New York, from Palisades
  Interstate Park Commission

26 Palisades Interstate Park Commission

26 L. F. Stockmeyer, from Palisades
  Interstate Park Commission

27 Palisades Interstate Park Commission

30 Roy Stevens, courtesy *Time*

32-33 Phelps Stokes Collection,
  New York Public Library

34-38 Courtesy of the
  Metropolitan Museum of Art

39-42 Sleepy Hollow Restorations

43 Buckingham

43 Gerald R. Watland

48 Hal and Margaret Nielson,
  from Shostal

50 W. H. Ballard

51 W. H. Ballard

51 National Park Service

52 Bettmann Archive

52-55 W. H. Ballard

56 G. and M. Heilman,
  from Shostal

57 National Park Service

58 W. H. Ballard

58 National Park Service

59 W. H. Ballard

59 National Park Service

62 Thomas Hollyman

64-65 National Park Service

66 Flournoy, Virginia State
  Chamber of Commerce

66-67 National Park Service

68 Nothman, from Monkmeyer

69 National Park Service

72 Ansel Adams

74-75 Jim Thompson

76 W. H. Purnell, from Shostal

77 Ansel Adams

77 National Park Service

78 Tennessee Conservation Dept.

79 Tennessee Conservation Dept.

79	Leon Kesteloo, from National Audubon Society	112	Alfred Eisenstaedt, courtesy *Life*
79	Tennessee Conservation Dept.	112	Frank and John Craighead (2)
80	Tennessee Conservation Dept.	113	Alfred Eisenstaedt, courtesy *Life*
80	Jim Thompson	116	Union Pacific Railroad Colorphoto
81	Tennessee Conservation Dept.	118	Ansel Adams
81	Jim Thompson	119	National Park Service
84	Fred Ragsdale, F. P. G.	120	Ansel Adams
86	Jesse Nusbaum, from Denver Public Library, Western History Dept.	122-125	National Park Service
87-89	Mason Weymouth, Brackman Associates	128	Ron Morrisette, from Jackson Hole Preserve
90-91	Frank Scherschel, courtesy *Life*	130-133	Fritz Henle, from Jackson Hole Preserve
		134-135	Ron Morrisette, from Jackson Hole Preserve
92-93	Mason Weymouth, Brackman Associates	136-139	Fritz Henle, from Jackson Hole Preserve
94	Alfred Eisenstaedt, courtesy *Life*	144	Ed Evans, from Shostal
95	Mason Weymouth, Brackman Associates	146	N. R. Farbman, courtesy *Life*
		147	Save-the-Redwoods League
96	Haynes Studios	148	Bettmann Archive
96-97	Mason Weymouth, Brackman Associates	148	Brown Brothers
		149	Brown Brothers
98-99	Haynes Studios	150	Save-the-Redwoods League
102	Alfred Eisenstaedt, courtesy *Life*	151	Collection of Horace M. Albright
104-105	Marion Carnahan, from Jackson Hole Preserve	151	Save-the-Redwoods League
		152	Raymond Moulin, National Geographic Society
106-107	National Park Service	153	Allan D. Cruikshank, from National Audubon Society (2)
108	Alfred Eisenstaedt, courtesy *Life*	153	Barron, Florida News Bureau
109	Alfred Eisenstaedt, courtesy *Life*	156	Thomas L. Williams, from Colonial Williamsburg
109	James R. Simon	158	Karsh, Ottawa
110	Pownall, from Jackson Hole Preserve	158-171	Colonial Williamsburg
111	From Jackson Hole Preserve	172	Dan Weiner
		173	Colonial Williamsburg
111	Pownall, from Jackson Hole Preserve	173	Karsh, Ottawa
		178	Laurance S. Rockefeller

The editorial research of this book was done by Helen M. Brown. Design and manufacturing production by L. J. Ansbacher and Staff, a Division of William E. Rudge's Sons: layout of photographs by William Mihalik, typography by Dorothy E. Barber; maps by David H. Greenspan. Type face throughout is English Monotype Times Roman. Process positives by Colorcraft Lithoplate Co.; offset presswork by The Meehan-Tooker Co.; gravure by Photogravure and Color Co.; text paper is Mohawk Paper Mills' *Superfine;* cover stock is Curtis Paper Company's *Tweedweave;* binding by Russell-Rutter Co.